J R Dewson.

Truman caused the title to be
changed after this edition came
out. He worked until he had
the auther to be kicked out.
When Prendergast died he flew
to see his old friend buried.
Prendergast was such a fine clean
up standing man.

Monroe, N.C.

"Life" From

Sirs:

. . . I do not believe the average man in this country was a friend of Pendergast. I do not believe the average man surrounds himself with a list of characters such as he has. If Truman is an average American the average certainly has gone down. . . .

Prairie View

MISSOURI WALTZ

MAURICE M. MILLIGAN

MISSOURI WALTZ

The Inside Story of the Pendergast Machine by the Man Who Smashed It

MAURICE M. MILLIGAN
Former U. S. District Attorney for the Western District of Missouri

CHARLES SCRIBNER'S SONS, NEW YORK
CHARLES SCRIBNER'S SONS, LTD., LONDON
1948

Printed in the United States of America

A

To Sue, my wife,
whose intelligence and
understanding kept me
on even keel when I
was in turbulent waters.

FOREWORD

I DESIRE here to pay tribute to the loyal and able members of my staff who stood shoulder to shoulder with me through the long and trying years of investigation and trial of cases that fell within the jurisdiction of the United States District Attorney's office. For the most part they were seasoned lawyers who stemmed from small towns in Missouri—"country lawyers" they called themselves.

Randall Wilson, my first assistant, came of an old family of lawyers. He was a veteran of the First World War and had served overseas as a Major. "The Skipper," as he was affectionately called, was a real battler in the courtroom.

Another stalwart was Sam C. Blair, also of a family of prominent lawyers, and whose father was a member of the Supreme Court of Missouri for a number of years. Sam has one of the most brilliant legal minds I have ever encountered. His unflagging energy in research and briefing of law cases greatly contributed to the success of our prosecutions.

Richard K. Phelps had been a school teacher. He served as a member of the Missouri State Legislature after taking his law degree. Phelps was not a dramatic or spectacular trial lawyer. He was a thorough workman, and his arguments were based on knowledge of the facts. His handling of these facts usually won the approbation of the jury.

Another assistant was Thomas A. Costellow, who was born and reared in the northern part of Missouri. He studied law at the University of Missouri, and was a member of the faculty of the Kansas City School of Law, where he taught Evidence.

To Otto Schmid was delegated the handling of our numerous routine cases while others of the staff gave almost full time to special matters. Born in Kansas City, Schmid received his education at Notre Dame and Harvard Universities. He faithfully and cheerfully rendered a most valuable service to the Government.

These men worked with me as a team, and rendered valuable aid in ridding Kansas City and Missouri of one of the most ruthless political machines that ever flourished in our nation. My debt to them is too great for me to repay with these few words of praise, but I want their names remembered as men who labored within the law to stamp out the evils of Pendergastism at a time when opposition to the Boss was looked upon as a hazardous occupation. Of the five, Randall Wilson has gone to his rest.

MAURICE M. MILLIGAN

KANSAS CITY, MO.

JANUARY 8, 1948

CONTENTS

MISSOURI WALTZ

PROLOGUE

Prologue

On January 26, 1945, Boss Tom Pendergast of Kansas City died a natural death and was given a decent funeral.

The Red Army was marching towards Berlin; General Douglas MacArthur was back in the Philippines, pushing the Japs towards Manila. Washington was buzzing with excitement, but the then Vice-President of the United States shoved his papers aside, boarded an Army bomber and flew to Kansas City to be present at Pendergast's funeral. "He was my friend, and I was his," he told reporters, and with these words Harry S. Truman affirmed his loyalty to the boss who had raised him to power.

This loyalty did not end at the bier, nor did it begin there. President Truman's continued affiliation with the political machine Pendergast constructed, and his close personal and political association with James Pendergast, the boss's nephew and political heir, have kept the founder's name alive. According to newspaper reports, James Pendergast is frequently a White House guest. He swims in the White House pool and accompanies the President on flights aboard the "Sacred Cow."

What was in the makeup of Tom Pendergast that commanded such loyalty, even in death? As a ruthless, calculating, ambitious, and powerful machine boss he had few equals and no superiors. Those who might have challenged his power were either afraid of him or were recipients of his favors. Others were so blindly loyal that, in their eyes, "the king could do no wrong." Almost any impartial account of Tom Pendergast will show him to be a complex person with all the exaggerated vices of a tyrant and with a touch of genius. The evil quality of that genius will, I believe, become more and more apparent as these pages unfold.

I

FORESHADOWS

Strictly Personal

I WANT to make it clear at the very outset that I am no novelist. I am a lawyer, and being a lawyer I am more concerned with facts than with fiction. I am not deluded by the legend that would make Boss Pendergast a friend and father to the poor, a man of incorruptible honor, and a victim of legal persecution, as his apologists, including President Truman, would have us believe. I know something about Pendergast. At one time my files bulged with information on him.

In every man's life certain years stand out in bold relief. For me 1934 was a landmark. On February 3, 1934, President Roosevelt appointed me United States District Attorney for the Western District of Missouri, a jurisdictional area comprising 66 of the 114 counties in the state, with Kansas City as headquarters.

Preceding the appointment I was called to Washington by Attorney General Homer S. Cummings for a conference. Actually, it was a screening, for during the conversation he inquired minutely into my personal history, and at times referred to a file on his desk. Mine was no routine appointment to pay a political debt. It became quite obvious that there was a job to be done in Kansas City and that the person assigned to it was expected to be free of organizational ties. The Attorney General bluntly asked me if I had any connections with any political organization in Kansas City.

Mr. Cummings said: "Kansas City is one of the three 'hot spots' in the United States. Chicago and St. Paul are the other two. These three cities have been linked in some manner with every kidnapping that has occurred to date, either as the *situs* of the crime, the hideout or the place of ransom payment. I want to appoint as District Attorney one who has no connection with any criminally-allied political organization and who will prosecute crime vigorously." I accepted that responsibility and that mandate. I replied that from my boyhood I had done what I could to advance the principles of the Democratic Party, but at no time had I ever joined any organization or association. My conscience was clear, and my hands were untied.

My fate was still undecided when I left the Attorney General's office. A lawyer from a neighboring county in Missouri was also being considered, and newspaper reporters allegedly wormed from the Attorney General's office a statement to the effect that my rival and I might have to shoot dice to determine the winner; the inference being that such methods were probably the ones the newsmen from Missouri could best understand.

I have a natural interest in the State of Missouri, for I was born and lived during the years of my youth on a farm adjoining the little town of Richmond, in Ray County, some forty miles northeast of Kansas City. Ray County could boast of many distinguished native and adopted sons. Colonel Alexander W. Doniphan of Mexican War fame, practiced law in Richmond. Austin A. King, one-time governor of Missouri, is buried there. In his early days the novelist James Lane Allen taught in the old Richmond College. Jacob T. Child served as minister to Siam and consul to China during Cleveland's two administrations. When the summer chautauqua came to town I heard men like William Jennings Bryan, Governor "Bob" Taylor, Opie Reed and other orators.

My father was active in local and state politics, although he never held an elective office in this solidly Democratic section. He loved politics for the sake of politics, and took an active part in elections. He often discussed political questions and situations with me as if I were an adult. I remember as a school boy, as I walked by the old courthouse in Richmond whose walls resounded with the heavy eloquence of the time, I would pause breathless with admiration while the sheriff would call from an upstairs window, "Lawyer Garner is wanted in the courtroom." Beginning at an early age I listened to many of the finest orators of the period.

Some of the early leaders of the Mormon Church lived in Richmond. Mormons still make pilgrimages to the town. The James boys and their gang had a secret hangout in Ray County; as a matter of fact their place of rendezvous was on a farm adjoining ours, but I never learned this until years later. My mother saw the James boys rob the Richmond bank. Jesse James was shot in St. Joseph, Missouri. Frank James lived to a ripe old age in a neighboring county.

I remember the Bryan campaign of 1896; the torchlight parades of marching members of the Kansas City

Flambeau Club; the skies reddened by flares of exploding Roman candles and skyrockets; the parade of men on horseback, one group of sixteen riding white horses accompanied by a lone horseman on the back of a beautiful sorrel stallion, illustrating the slogan: "Free and unlimited coinage of silver at the ratio of sixteen silver dollars to one of gold."

Another incident that stands out in my memory is a chance encounter with Robert M. LaFollette of Wisconsin, known then as "Fighting Bob." He had come to Richmond in 1912 to make a speech. Being a great admirer of his, after the speech I saw him sitting on the courthouse steps and was emboldened to introduce myself, hoping to get a few words from him. To my surprise and very great pleasure he talked to me for several hours. I have forgotten a great deal of what he said, but I can still recall these words he spoke as we sat on the steps of the deserted courthouse under a warm Missouri moon. "Young man," he said, "take the side of the people. It's the right side. It's not only the right side, it's the winning side." Contrast this with Tom Pendergast's observation: "There are always three sides to any question—your side, my side, and the right side."

As a boy I was permitted to recess my schooling temporarily so that I might serve as a clerk in the State Senate during the sessions of the legislature. In the environment of Jefferson City I became thoroughly a victim of the virus of politics. I was rather fortunate in being a namesake and friend of the leader of the State Senate, and thereby had the run of his office and hotel apartment where gathered from time to time most of the leading political lights of the state, from the governor on down. I was permitted to sit in, or, to be more exact, my presence was ignored, at these meetings. With the *Bible* in one hand and *Blackstone* in the other, these worthies could talk down Demosthenes himself. I kept silent and listened. Being young and strictly brought up I could do nothing else.

Bathtubs were not common in this period and the Saturday night bath was not just a cue from Mr. Bones to Mr. Interlocutor. One of my close friends in Jefferson City was the deputy clerk of the Supreme Court, and at his invitation I retired each Saturday night to the old Supreme Court building to use one of the bathtubs provided each of the Supreme Court Justices in their private chambers. My friend and I had a ritual which never varied on these occasions. As I would enter his office in the building, after exchanging the usual pleasantries he would say, "Well, whose bathtub will it be tonight?" I would pretend to give the matter deep thought and he would say, "Judge Gantt wrote a good opinion this week," and I would reply, "I think I'll try his tub," and into these sanctums of judicial plumbing I would retire.

In the lobby of the old Madison Hotel I used to listen by the hour to that doughty old political warrior, Colonel John T. Crisp, of Jackson County. If the Colonel lacked a grown-up audience I pushed myself into the nearest chair and sat for hours as he poured forth his philosophy of life.

While attending high school in Richmond I read *Blackstone* on the side, along with other law books. As a result of this I was admitted to the practice of law the Monday morning following the Friday evening graduation ceremonies at the high school. I guarded this secret of my previous admission to the bar during the years that followed as a law student at the University of Missouri. No classmate learned of this until the members of the class had to appear before the Supreme Court Commission and pass the rugged test of the State bar examination.

Upon my graduation from the University of Missouri I returned to Richmond and began the practice of law. Tradition imposed upon me the prospect of a "starvation period" of at least five years. I happily circumvented this by getting myself elected City Attorney, which office carried with it a monthly remuneration and a stipulated fee for each conviction in the City Court of violation of the ordinances. Following this I was elected Judge of the Probate Court. The title of "Judge" made me feel somewhat older, but I was informed that I was the youngest man, up to that time, to be elected Judge of the Probate Court in the whole State of Missouri.

My younger brother, Jacob L. Milligan, shared my law office with me. When the First World War broke out he helped organize a volunteer company in Ray County and spent many months in France as its Captain. Many of the boys in old "Company G," boys I had known for years, never came back. When "Tuck," as all the local folks called my brother, returned, there happened to be a vacancy in our Congressional district. "Tuck" was asked to run, and after a hard political battle, was elected. He served in the National House of Representatives for thirteen years. His wartime buddy, Senator Bennett C. Clark, presented my name when a successor to William L. Vandeventer, U. S. District Attorney, was being sought.

I DISCOVER THE MEANING OF HOT SPOT

WHEN I walked out of the office of Attorney General Cummings his words kept running through my head. "Kansas City is one of the three hot spots in the United States." How hot it really was I was soon to learn. My appointment was confirmed in that exciting year of 1934, and I took up my headquarters in Kansas City. I cannot escape the impression that my appearance on the scene was looked upon by many people acquainted with the Pendergast machine as just another dull chapter in the long story of timid assault and hasty retreat. Messages of congratulation poured in, my close friends wished me luck, but the big question remained unanswered. Would the Federal government step in where local and State governments feared to tread?

I took over the office of U. S. District Attorney with a firm determination to enforce the Federal statutes, come what may, but little did I realize what the future held in the way of political drama. Things began to happen before I had a chance to catch my breath, and they kept on happening month after month. It was as though someone had touched off a fuse, and one explosive charge set off the charge just ahead of it, and each explosion was louder than the preceding one. Looking back at those years, I often wonder how my aides and I stood the strain of so many legal battles coming in such rapid succession. We learned at first hand what the Attorney General meant when he used the expression "hot spot."

In 1934 Kansas City was sizzling, and I am not speaking of the weather.

I had always lived close enough to Kansas City to know something about its political issues. I had followed the fights between the "Goats" and the "Rabbits" over the years, and I knew something about Boss Pendergast. I was not altogether ignorant of the positions occupied in the Pendergast empire by City Manager McElroy and the shadowy racketeer, Johnny Lazia. I did not need to be told that Kansas City's police setup was rotten, that crime was rampant, and that vice was flourishing. Justice, on anything less than a Federal scale seemed blind or inept, or both. I disavow any originality for that statement. The whole problem was very convincingly outlined by Raymond Moley and others in the *Missouri Crime Survey*[1] as early as 1926.

The same Raymond Moley, writing in the magazine *Today*, June 30, 1934 (the very year I took over my job in Kansas City) said: "Ten years ago I participated in a survey of crime in the State of Missouri, made under the auspices of a group of public-minded lawyers headed by Guy A. Thompson, since president of the American Bar Association. I said then '. . . the margin of safety offered the professional criminal by our (Missouri) machinery for law enforcement is very large, so large, in fact, that the criminal profession is not unduly hazardous. The chances are mostly in favor of the professional criminal . . . the machinery of justice is too cumbersome; there is too little coordination and cooperation among the

[1] Missouri Association for Criminal Justice, *Missouri Crime Survey*, New York. The Macmillan Company, 1926.

various agencies working to the same end . . . there is laxity in prosecutions; and there is altogether too much leniency exhibited in the granting of pardons, paroles and commutations.' In a measurable degree the survey stimulated public opinion in various parts of the state, and a number of desirable gains were made. But the solid control of Kansas City by a 'practical political machine' then, as now, under Boss Pendergast, kept Kansas City immune from the influence towards reform."

I soon found out that the above indictment of a corrupt machine was an understatement. Kansas City was in the center of a crime corridor that stretched from St. Paul to the Southwest. Criminals fleeing from the ends of the corridor found refuge, as well as protection, in the center. The hardened eastern thugs avoided the corridor. They were not tough enough for membership in the Kansas City fraternity. Life was cheap in those days. Gang victims were tossed off bridges dressed in concrete bathing suits. It was the kidnapping era. The expression "Public Enemy Number One" gained currency, and the youngsters forsook the beloved cowboy roles to play the part of "G-Men."

Johnny Lazia's name kept creeping into the news. By virtue of his friendship with Pendergast he seemed to be a privileged character. He honored certain "social" events with his presence, he advised the Chief of Police on matters pertaining to the underworld, he acted as liaison between Pendergast and some of the politicians in "Little Italy." The passport to success in the gambling world was the simple statement, "I know Johnny Lazia." Lazia took his regular cut in the manifold gambling rackets, and was master of the "fix." The income from one of these rackets was estimated by agents of the Government to be approximately two million dollars a year. His other "takes" added more millions of dollars annually. The individual operators of these rackets paid a percentage of their profits to a regular collector designated by Lazia. A similar toll was levied upon vice in the same fashion. Some of the gambling joints flourished within a block or two of Kansas City's highly respectable shopping district. People paid little attention to infractions of the ordinances. Gamblers walked out to lunch wearing their green aprons and eyeshades. They did not wish to take the few minutes necessary to remove them.

Edward Morrow, writing in the Omaha *World Herald,* said: "If you want to see some sin, forget about Paris and go to Kansas City. With the possible exception of such renowned centers as Singapore and Port Said, Kansas City probably has the greatest sin industry in the world." Describing the "red light" district on 14th Street the same writer observed: "The street was lined with dreary flats. In every window, upstairs and down, were women. Some knitted, some read, some sewed. Bright lights, in some cases bordering the windows, lighted the women's faces . . . When the cab drew near the women dropped what they had in their hands, seized nickels and began to tap furiously on the window pane. A steady drum of tapping accompanied the cab up the street. We swung into a street where most of the window tappers were Japanese."

Fred Allhoff, writing in *Liberty* magazine, confirms the above and more besides. "Kansas City has three hundred churches and heaven knows how many gambling joints, at least one of which advertises regularly in the newspapers. You can name your games and stakes in dozens of wide-open gambling halls, in some cases operated or partially controlled by ex-election judges, ex-precinct captains, and ex-convicts; by relatives of police officers, garbage inspectors, assistant prosecuting attorneys, and other fair-haired favorites of the machine. Prostitution and gambling are the oil that runs the machine that runs a great city. An oil made all the more effective by the fact that when you toss your cash on a Kansas City gaming table you are pitting it against marked cards, marked and crooked dice."[1]

This was the rich field staked out by Johnny Lazia, friend of Pendergast and Police Chief Otto Higgins. Lazia's power was illustrated by a murder committed in the summer of 1933. Sheriff Thomas B. Bash, an honest and courageous public official, accompanied by his wife and small child and one of his deputies, was returning home at night from a Sunday afternoon outing in the country. About midnight he reached a street intersection that runs into Armour Boulevard, a much-traveled and well-lighted thoroughfare in Kansas City. Hearing shots fired across the street, the sheriff stopped his car, grabbed a riot gun from its rack and jumped out of the car to investigate, followed by his deputy. Their attention was immediately attracted to a car which was being driven slowly in their direction, and to a man who was running towards them. Suddenly the occupants of the moving car began shooting at the sheriff, who in turn opened fire on

[1] *Liberty.* Sept. 17, 1938.

them, and the car careened into the curb and came to a standstill.

The man in the street continued his approach, firing at the sheriff until that officer turned his gun on him. Immediately his assailant dropped his weapon and screamed, "Don't shoot! I'm a friend of Johnny Lazia!"

After placing his quarry under arrest, Sheriff Bash investigated and discovered that two of the men in the fugitive car had been killed, apparently victims of his *own* gunfire. Across the street he saw the riddled body of a man lying prone upon the pavement and bearing mute testimony of gang warfare. City officers had reached the scene by this time and further examination of the premises continued.

The sheriff, retaining possession of the gun dropped by the man, later identified as Charles Gargotta, loaded his assailant into a police car and took him to the county jail. On the way there the prisoner, pointing to a gun concealed on his person, said to an officer, "You had better take this gun." A search of the surroundings near the scene of the crime revealed another gun lying a short distance away. This weapon was picked up by a city police officer and turned over to one Leonard Claiborne, a detective of the Kansas City Police Department. The latter gun was taken to police headquarters and turned over for laboratory examination.

Out of this fatal melee three guns had been discovered, all similar in make and caliber, a rather baffling and strange coincidence. The pistol dropped by Gargotta together with the one taken from him in the ride to the bastille, were duly tagged for identification by the sheriff and agents of the Federal Bureau of Investigation, and in turn presented to a private expert in ballistics.

These guns bearing the serial numbers 377675 and 69791 were guns possessed by Gargotta; the gun later picked up near the place of the murder by police officer Strean and turned over to Claiborne bore serial number 504567. According to the report of the expert on ballistics, following examination and tests made in firing the same and the comparison with bullets taken from the bodies of the victim, the murder weapon was positively identified as the Gargotta gun No. 377675, dropped by him before being taken into custody by the sheriff.

Gargotta was summarily charged with first degree murder in the State Court. Here, it seemed, was an airtight case; the defendant caught red-handed running from the scene of the crime, carrying in hand the tell-tale murder weapon which had blazed away at an officer of the law. But lurking behind the curtain of justice was Pendergast's lieutenant ready to do battle for one of the boys—the same Johnny Lazia who had placed many of his trusted friends on the police force.

When the day of the trial came on, among the witnesses appearing for the State of Missouri in the prosecution was detective Claiborne, who said that he had tagged the gun given to him by police officer Strean, which Strean had found some distance away from the scene of the shooting. This gun, Claiborne testified, bore the serial number 377675 and offered as supporting evidence a small red tag labeled in his handwriting bearing the 377675, dated August 12, 1933, and containing thereon his own initials as marks of identification. According to

Claiborne's testimony, neither gun found in Gargotta's possession could be the fatal weapon but on the contrary the gun found by Strean must have been the murder weapon. This testimony so confused the issues of the trial that the jury returned a verdict of not guilty. Gargotta walked out of court a free man so far as the cold-blooded killing of Ferris Anthon was concerned. Anthon was the gangland victim found at the scene of the crime by Sheriff Bash.

It was reported that the friends of Gargotta were arranging a celebration for him the evening following the jury's verdict. But it so happened that the three guns involved in the homicide were Army pistols recently stolen from a Government arsenal at Kansas City, Kansas, and were the property of the United States. This fact alone gave the Federal Government jurisdiction. I immediately stepped in and put my men to work on the case. Before the scheduled festivities celebrating Gargotta's escape from the clutches of the law could be launched, Gargotta was apprehended and brought before the Federal Court, charged with possessing and concealing two stolen 45 caliber automatic pistols bearing the serial numbers 377675 and 69791. A Federal Grand Jury was summoned and it began an intensive investigation of the whole matter.

Leonard Claiborne, who had served the State so "faithfully" in the recent trial, was hailed before the jury. The little "red tag" was impounded as evidence and scrutinized for any hidden testimony it might have concealed. During the inquiry one of my assistants made a hurried trip east to Framingham, Massachusetts, to inspect the records of the Dennison Manufacturing Company from which the tag had been purchased. This tag contained the inscription or legend "10 M 5-2-33" in small print, the name of the manufacturer, etc.

Detective Claiborne, being called before the Grand Jury for testimony, related the same story he had given in court during the Gargotta trial—how he had made out this "tag" on the date of August 12, 1933, and inscribed the serial number of the gun 377675. He was recalled by the jury, and again and again was prevailed upon to reiterate his testimony as to filling in data on the tag.

My assistant returned meanwhile with conclusive proof and record-evidence obtained from the Dennison Manufacturing Company showing that the "red tag" was not even made in the factory until October 27, 1933,—exactly two months and fifteen days after August 12, 1933, the day Claiborne said he filled in the tag with the data on the gun. The notation "10 M 5-2-33" was not the date it was made, but was the date the city ordered ten thousand tags from the company.

Claiborne was immediately indicted by the Grand Jury for perjury and later brought to trial, convicted and sentenced to four years in the penitentiary. Why had Claiborne falsified the records in order to protect Gargotta? E. E. Conroy, one of the crack Special Agents of the FBI, who arrested Claiborne, got the answer through patient and adroit questioning. Claiborne confessed that Johnny Lazia had been responsible for his testimony in regard to the gun. "I am not in the Army," Claiborne told Conroy, "but I have to take orders." The little "red tag" played a dual role in the tragedy of guns. It freed Gargotta from the murder charge, but by a quirk of fate it made a felon of detective Claiborne.

In regard to Claiborne's indictment on a perjury charge the Kansas City *Star* editorialized: "At Last, a Perjury Indictment!" Note the exclamation point. The editorial concluded: "The laxness with which perjury has been regarded has tended to make it a major element in defeating justice in Kansas City. The mere fact that a trial for perjury is to be held will prove a salutary and a needed lesson in this community."

What happened to Gargotta? He was brought to trial again, defended for the most part by the same legal counsel that had defended Claiborne, was convicted and sentenced to three years in the penitentiary, the maximum punishment, but he gained his freedom again through a majority opinion of the Circuit Court of Appeal upon the ground that the evidence against him was insufficient to sustain the verdict of guilty. As an ironic sidelight to this decision it might be interesting to know that after many continuances covering a period of years, Gargotta was finally brought to trial in the State Court and admitted his guilt to the charge that he committed felonious assault on Sheriff Thomas B. Bash on the date of August 12, 1933. By this plea he admitted the possession of the stolen automatic No. 377675 as charged in the Federal prosecution.

The public did not seem to be very much interested in the crime situation in Kansas City. It did not know that more than sixty ex-convicts had been placed on the police payroll at the request of Johnny Lazia. In 1934 one-tenth of the entire police force in Kansas City had criminal records. I was amazed at this public apathy. There had been sporadic attempts to eradicate some of the evils in the body politic, but no general uprising. I am of the firm conviction that an aroused citizenry in any community, working as one mighty instrument of justice, can bring any boss to his knees.

I remember the indignation on the part of some citizens when a former Kansas Citian wrote a magazine article in which he portrayed Kansas City as corrupt and contented, using the same words Lincoln Steffens had employed in the "muckraking" era in describing boss-ridden Philadelphia. I also recall the visit of a nationally known columnist. He made a tour of the gambling and vice dens, escorted by the then Chief of Police. His syndicated column published in the Kansas City papers the following morning failed to cause a single ripple of protest on the part of outraged citizens. They accepted the insidious germs in the political bloodstream with the same complacency they accepted the common cold—leave it alone and it would cure itself. But it didn't. It got progressively worse.

This was the Kansas City I came to know in the early months of 1934. I could not understand how a city of beautiful homes, an imposing art center, with splendid public buildings, spacious parks and playgrounds, and other marks of culture and beauty could exist side by side with a corrupt machine run by a boss like Pendergast. Pendergast was no patron of the arts—he was a patron of the race tracks. Lazia was Italian, but he was no Lorenzo the Magnificent. Kansas City was a beautiful place because men and women of imperishable ideals made it so by the sovereign power of their dreams. They made it so in spite of Pendergast. I want the reader to understand this. Pendergast, the man, notwithstanding the apologies of some of his more distinguished followers, was an overbearing, ruthless, calculating public enemy, and his political machine was a vicious, criminal conspiracy.

THE BOSS: A LONG-RANGE VIEW

THE stranger to the ways of the West may wonder, as he hears the recital of Pendergast's record of vicious bossism, how the decent people of Kansas City put up with him for so many years. Why was he not curbed before he got complete control of the city? That is an academic question. One might as well say, "Why did the people of Germany put up with Hitler?" I think it can be said without exaggeration that the people of Kansas City accepted Pendergast as the visible symbol of their pragmatic philosophy of live-and-let-live. They took a certain amount of pride in him. If Kansas City had to have a boss (and there were plenty of solid citizens who saw certain advantages in such a system of government), let him be the most colorful, the most powerful, the most feared boss in the United States . . . something big like the Union Station, the Liberty Memorial, the stockyards, Convention Hall, or Swope Park! It seems absurd, on the face of it, to accuse a city of glorifying its own political corruption, but that is exactly what Kansas City did. Pendergast made headlines. He was front page copy. There is always some big civic organization to beat the drum for a Huey Long, a Mayor

Hague, or a Tom Pendergast. How explain this phenomenon except as a perverted manifestation of unreasoning local pride?

Pendergast ruled his empire from a shabby, bare, unpretentious office at 1908 Main Street, in the business section of Kansas City. It was a bit on the ordinary side. He sat behind an old-fashioned roll top desk, and always wore his hat. The furnishings were plain. You could get no indication of the man's taste from this room; it was purely functional. On the wall was an old newspaper cartoon showing his brother Jim holding a ballot box in his hands. On and in his desk were photographs of his family. Guarding his private office from the outside stood a 6 foot, 3 inch, well-built, erect man with a courteous manner, a retired river boat captain, Elijah Matheus. This unusual-looking character ushered in the visitors, ranging from governors to gunmen; from bankers to bums. Rank meant nothing in Pendergast's waiting room. Tom never came through the waiting room himself, he entered his private office through a secret entrance. Dignitaries often squirmed in the hard chairs in the outer office while some lowly ward heeler poured out his tale of woe to the boss.

Pendergast made it a point to see as many people as he could. He wanted to know what was going on in each precinct in Kansas City and in each county in Missouri. He was always on the alert against being double-crossed or having someone cut into his territory. He loved power and would tolerate no rival. His interviews were of a legendary brevity. Tom was an excellent listener as long as one talked about the business at hand, and his clear, strong, unwavering grey eyes seldom left his visitor. However, he tolerated little palaver about the weather. His cryptic "yes" or "no" carried finality, and the legend that "Tom's word is as good as his bond," was carefully nurtured. That moth-eaten cliché runs through the annals of bossism. It lacks originality, and is beginning to run thin.

Pendergast demanded and received unwavering loyalty. He had his own special treatment for ingrates. He was powerful because he had a massive political machine of unchallenged power behind him. Make no mistake—this organization could do more than elect or defeat candidates for political office. It could make or break a business through tax levies, building permits, building condemnations by city inspectors, special favors, and in a hundred other ways. Patronage—jobs—were dispensed to friends of the organization, not its enemies. Pendergast had merely to pick up the telephone on his desk and things would begin to happen very quickly in Washington or Jefferson City, the capital of Missouri. The influential citizens were not blind. They knew the Pendergast machine was corrupt and that it ran Kansas City. But, in what appears to be the American tradition, they said, "I've got my business to run and I'm not interested in politics anyway." As long as the machine helped or at least tolerated their existence they maintained a discreet silence.

Pendergast precinct captains clothed the needy and fed the poor. A new family moving into Kansas City was immediately paid a visit by a precinct captain. "May I get the gas turned on for you, Mrs. Smith?" "Yes sir, Mr. Smith, I'll have that water turned on for you the first thing in the morning." Unless the Smiths requested further favors of this precinct captain, his next visit would take place on registration day a few days before the next election. The Pendergast philosophy was simple: put a man under obligation to you and he will work for you on election day. Not that all votes were ever legally counted as cast. If the honest votes were not enough to swing an election the machine could always come up with the necessary quota of dishonest votes. It made no difference in the end. Pendergast candidates always won.

This was the man I had to lick. Let us probe a little into his past, and into the origins of his political machine, in order to trace the historical process whereby such a man came to rule a great American city.

II

TALE OF TWO CITIES

Roots in St. Joe

TOM PENDERGAST'S parents, Michael and Mary Pendergast, were natives of Tipperary, Ireland. Like a great many other sons and daughters of Erin they came to America in the hope of finding economic security in a young country filled with opportunity. Michael and Mary Pendergast settled in Gallipolis, Ohio, and in 1856 a son was born to them, and they named him James. In 1857 the Pendergasts pushed westward, but they got no farther than St. Joseph, Missouri. They entered the town in a wagon, for as yet St. Joe (Missourians always use this shorter name) had no railroads. But the railroads were on their way, and that may have been a factor affecting Michael Pendergast's decision to remain there. He was a teamster and St. Joe was a teamster's paradise, thanks to the freighting firm of Russell, Majors and Waddell. The fact that the little river settlement was named after a saint was accepted as a good omen, for the Pendergasts were Catholics. Joseph Roubidoux, who founded the town in 1826, was a Catholic, as was Fred Smith, who platted and recorded the site under the name of St. Joseph in 1843. Originally, it had been called Blacksnake Hills after a tribe of Indians of that name.

Those were pioneer days. It should be remembered that

Tom Pendergast's life spanned a period of western development that saw St. Joseph rise from nothing, become a flourishing center of trade and then decline in importance, while Kansas City grew from a Missouri River landing to a populous city with a network of railroads that opened up the Southwest.

One event will serve to illustrate the pioneer aspect of St. Joseph. It took place three years after Tom Pendergast's parents had arrived there. The local firm of Russell, Majors and Waddell, mentioned above, contracted with the Government to deliver the transcontinental mail and express in record time. To achieve this they proposed a plan whereby the distance between St. Joseph, Missouri, and Sacramento, California, was to be covered by relays of the Pony Express. This service was inaugurated in St. Joseph, April 3, 1860.

The whole town turned out for the opening trumpet blast which was to send the first rider galloping westward. Sensing the historical importance of the occasion the crowd surrounded the pony and rider and plucked nearly all the hairs from the pony's tail, souvenirs to hand down from father to son. At the appointed hour the rider dashed down the hill to the ferry, crossed the wide Missouri and was on his perilous way. The Pony Express riders carried Colt revolvers and Spencer rifles. Among the crack shots assigned to this venture were Buffalo Bill, Pony Bob, John Fry, Bill Baker and Jack Slade. Slade later became an outlaw. The boys who grew up in Tom Pendergast's generation knew the exploits of these men by heart.

The Pony Express broke all records for speed. Lincoln's

inaugural address was carried from St. Joseph to Sacramento in seven days and seventeen hours, a record, and it thrilled a young and boastful nation. It was a glamorous page in our history, but it bankrupted Russell, Majors and Waddell. To maintain 80 riders, 500 horses, 400 station employees, and 190 relay stations involved too much overhead. The failure of this great firm was a severe blow to St. Joseph at the time, but the coming of the "Iron Horse" more or less made up for the loss. The Pony Express was a last magnificent and romantic gesture of the Wild West. The Machine Age was moving across the continent. The herds of buffalo disappeared from the plains, the Indians were pushed back into their reservations, and the ominous sound of the train whistle was heard.

Michael Pendergast, teamster, witnessed this transition. He saw the collapse of the empire constructed by Russell, Majors and Waddell. It is difficult to comprehend the magnitude of this firm's operations. At one time it used 75,000 head of oxen, 1,000 mules, 6,000 teamsters and 6,200 wagons! "Such acres of wagons!" exclaimed Horace Greeley, looking over the firm's field headquarters at Leavenworth, Kansas. Yet within three years this gigantic enterprise was but a memory.

The Pendergasts lived on Frederick Avenue, an old stagecoach road that cut diagonally across St. Joseph. In this Frederick Avenue home was born Thomas Joseph Pendergast, July 22, 1872. The *St. Joseph Gazette* records that the temperature on that particular day reached 93 degrees in the shade. The heat was followed by a tempestuous storm. The same issue of the *Gazette* mentioned that the grand jury had returned seven bills of indictment, a man fell from the second story window in Mr. Riley's saloon, injuring himself with broken glass, the Union Baseball Club was organized. Oddly enough, baseball, saloons and indictments were to figure prominently in Tom Pendergast's life. He was born under a dark cloud and he died under one.

St. Joseph is likely to remember the year 1872 for more important events than the one just recorded. It was the year Milton Tootle opened Tootle's Opera House, called "the finest west of Chicago," which it was. The opening program featured Maggie Mitchell, starring in a performance of "Fanchon." This was the year that the author of "Little Boy Blue" came to St. Joe to pay court to pretty Julia Comstock and to ride with her down a street near the Pendergast home known to this day as Lovers' Lane. Eugene Field used this incident in a poem he wrote later that same year. It was in 1872 that the piers for the railroad bridge across the Missouri were laid. The bridge was officially opened the following year with a celebration unsurpassed in the town's history, fifty thousand people participating. A six-mile long parade was a feature, Japanese lanterns blinked at night, and the Germans of the Northwest held their annual "Saengerfest" in St. Joseph the very day of the bridge opening.

People were already calling St. Joseph "Porkopolis" in imitation of Cincinnati, for the year Tom Pendergast was born the local meat packers processed 93,000 hogs. One finds in the city directories of that day that St. Joseph boasted of three portrait painters, two string bands, two bathrooms, and ninety saloons. Those were the good old days of "Uncle John" Abel's Pacific Hotel, the Emmet Guards, Pryor's Military Band, Studebaker's "gentlemen's buggies," Goetz Beer and Westheimer Brothers' "Native American Stomach Bitters."

Photographers were called Ambrotype or Daguerrean Artists. Alex Lozo and Spencer Landon were doing "tintypes" when Tom Pendergast was dressed up for his first picture. "Lovers of Fashion" patronized William Eckhart at the Sign of the Golden 8 on Felix Street. Newby's Hoop Skirt Factory did a good business. There was no lack of entertainment in St. Joe, ranging from the St. Joseph Theatre where Miss Breslaw was a "fixed star" to "Varieties —an institution where there is good dancing, questionable singing and a scarcity of crinoline amongst the women." The world's oldest profession flourished in certain sections of town. It was a rip-roaring era of lawlessness all up and down the Missouri-Kansas Border, an era that gave rise to the James boys.

When Tom Pendergast reached the proper age he was sent to a parochial school. His parents enrolled him in St. Patrick's at the corner of Eleventh and Monterey Streets. During 1884-1885 Tom Pendergast had progressed to a point in this school which we would rank today as being equivalent to the sophomore class in high school. At this date Brother Marcellian was in charge.

All the writers who have gone into the subject of Tom Pendergast's life mention, as though it were a fact, his attendance at St. Mary's College, St. Mary's, Kansas, where he was reputedly a star baseball player. There is no record of Thomas J. Pendergast's attendance there. A search made revealed not a trace of Pendergast's stay at St. Mary's College. No list in the printed catalogues and no registration book yielded results. In the rough and tumble of ward politics a college degree would have been no asset. The voters are often suspicious of any educational attainments above their own. The number of intellectuals in the annals of bossism is small.

This attitude towards scholarship is illustrated by a remark once made by "Colonel" Butler, well-known political boss of St. Louis. He was in Columbia, Missouri, seat of the University of Missouri, facing trial, due to a sudden change of venue. Walking about the town and sizing it up, the "Colonel" asked a local resident, "Sir, what's the main business here?" The native, with a mingled touch of pride and astonishment, replied, "Education," and pointed to the campus. "That's a hell of a business!" the boss snorted, and strode on.

In 1882, when Pendergast was ten years old, the bank robber Jesse James, then living in St. Joe under the name of Thomas Howard, was shot in the back by Bob Ford, one of his former confederates. The date was April 3, and spring flowers were coming up in the yard which held the little white cottage with the green shutters—the Jesse James house at 1318 Lafayette Street. Tom Pendergast and his pals knew the spot well. On one of his last trips to St. Joe, Pendergast told a reporter about such incidents and he remembered the names of all the boys he used to play with, even knew what became of them. Jesse James and Tom Pendergast have at least one thing in common. Both figure prominently in the controversial mural by Thomas Hart Benton in the State Capitol at Jefferson City, Missouri.

The Pendergast story as far as St. Joseph is concerned may be summed up briefly. Tombstone inscriptions in Mt. Olivet Cemetery at Twenty-fifth and Lovers' Lane read:

> Michael Pendergast. Born 1826-Died 1893
> Mary Pendergast. Born 1834-Died Dec. 30, 1902
> Mary Pendergast Costello. Born 1859-Died Aug. 29, 1938
> Delia and Catherine Pendergast (buried in the same grave and with no dates given.)

Michael and Mary, of course, were Tom Pendergast's parents. Mary (Mrs. William C. Costello), Delia and Catherine, were his sisters. Besides the above, there were: James, Michael J., John, Josephine (Pendergast) Moore, and Margaret (Pendergast) Klingbeil. We shall meet some of them again in Kansas City.

Tom Pendergast was a young man when he left St. Joseph. Charles Barnett, an old resident, still remembers him as he was at that time. "I was a street car conductor. Tom often rode in my trolley car. He was a friendly and good-natured boy. I liked him." Julius Grasloff, who lived next door to the Pendergasts, said substantially the same thing when my investigator interviewed him. Lee Van Vickle, monument dealer, who now owns the old Pendergast property at 1715 Frederick Avenue, lived until October, 1946, in the house where Tom Pendergast was born. On that date he had it torn down in order to use the lot as a place of display for his monuments. He did not look upon it as a shrine.

K. C.

THE tall memorial shaft that stands high above the Union Station Plaza in Kansas City catches and holds the eye of the visitor. It is like a giant exclamation point set on a hill. It records the upward groping of the human spirit in search of something more enduring than stockyards.

Kansas City needs such a symbol. It helps her forget those bloodstains on the Station Plaza below. There, on a June morning in 1933, four officers of the law were murdered in cold blood by gangsters armed with machine guns. In the annals of the FBI that crime will always be known as the Union Station Massacre, and of it we shall hear more.

Kansas City must plead guilty to turning out *en masse* for the funeral of her gaudiest racketeer, John Lazia, friend of Pendergast. She must plead guilty to tolerating elections degraded by the presence of armed bands of thugs cruising the streets in cars bearing no license plates.

A city of art and enterprise, but one bearing the ugly scars of Boss Pendergast's corrupt political machine.

Throughout her turbulent history Missouri's second largest city (with a consuming ambition to be first) has been a battleground of conflicting forces. Even as far back as the Civil War she was torn between the North and the South.

Born in a bend of the Missouri River where the muddy waters turn eastward and say farewell to the West, Kansas City has her feet in the mud and her head among the stars—a city of corruption and aspiration. Only on her lofty bluffs were settlers safe from floods.

She has always had her star-gazers. Take J. C. Nichols, who filled her cow pastures with beautiful homes and statuary imported from Italy, and who is now trying to make her a center of scientific research; take the Quaker, Kersey Coates, who built an imposing opera house and set the tone for "Quality Hill"; or take William Rockhill Nelson, art lover and crusading editor and owner of the *Kansas City Star,* who preached the gospel of beauty to stubborn materialists.

The Pendergast saga belongs to the muddy side. Year after year it was Tom Pendergast, the saloon keeper grown great, the stuffer of ballot boxes, the "Big Shot" with the neck of a bull who relaxed his 250 pounds between sheets that matched the color scheme of his bedroom, who piped the tune that Kansas City danced to.

That is the chapter that hurts.

With the world grown so small it seems hardly necessary to fix the geographical location of Kansas City, but many people think that this great industrial center in the "Heart of America" is in Kansas. Perhaps a bit of history is in order.

In the beginning Kansas City was called Chouteau's Landing. Later it was called Westport Landing, even though the town of Westport itself was a few miles to the south on the dusty Santa Fe Trail, choked with covered wagons and the commerce of the plains. John C. McCoy, the founder of Westport, wanted an outlet to navigable water, so he and his associates carved a sort of "Polish Corridor" through the hills, woods and ravines and called the wharf at the northern end of it Westport Landing. It was a place where steamboats came to unload cargo and to pick up more—just a jumping-off place, with ravines and gullies serving as roads for creaking ox-carts, and paths running through dense patches of evil-smelling jimson weeds and the even more pungent dog fennel which always seems to follow poor farmers from East to West. To coax an ox through that wilderness and up those precipitous bluffs required a picturesque vocabulary, one heavily weighted with profanity. To this day the descendants of those hardy pioneers retain some of the rugged expressions that used to bounce off the side of those hills like buckshot.

In 1872, the year of Tom Pendergast's birth, John C. McCoy, looking back on those early days in Westport Landing, spoke of "an old log house on the river bank occupied by a lank, cadaverous specimen of humanity named Ellis, with one blind eye and the other on the lookout for stray horses, straggling Indians, and squatters with whom to swap a tin cup of whiskey for a coon skin." He also mentioned the French trappers living in the Kaw bottomlands, "engaged principally in raising young half breeds."

Someone suggested that the place be called Kawsmouth, since the Kansas River (called Kaw by the French *voyageurs*) challenged the mighty Missouri for the right-of-way at this point. The name was descriptive, but it did not gain favor. Finally, a meeting was held in the cabin of "One-Eyed" Ellis for the purpose of selecting a suitable name for the settlement. Webster's *Blue Backed Speller* was consulted, and a number of names were read off. Squire Bowers suggested that the place be called "Rabbitville" or "Possum-trot," but this facetious recommendation was greeted with silent contempt.

On February 4, 1850, this name-seeking community was incorporated as the Town of Kansas—the beginning of geographical confusion. In 1853 it was changed to City of Kansas, which proves that there must have been some potential chamber of commerce men around even at that early date. It was a highly presumptuous name since the settlement was neither a city nor in Kansas, but it looked imposing in the railroad literature of the day, and served as bait for eastern capitalists with money to invest.

The very year that the name City of Kansas was adopted, the Missouri statesman, Thomas Hart Benton, stood on the site and with a majestic wave of the hand to punctuate his florid oratory exclaimed: "There, gentlemen, where the rocky bluff meets and turns aside the sweeping current of this mighty river . . . a large commercial and manufacturing community will congregate, and less than a generation will see a great city on these hills." He was right.

Another Thomas Hart Benton stood on these same bluffs a few years ago and reflected upon the shabby treatment accorded his murals in the Missouri State Capitol. I have mentioned the fact that Benton stuck Pendergast in one of the murals to symbolize the politician. The people of Kansas City were a bit touchy on this matter. It would remind posterity of a rather shameful page of her history.

In 1889 the name City of Kansas was turned around and Kansas City, Missouri, has been the correct designation ever since. Not to be outdone, the town of Wyandotte on the banks of the Kaw changed its name to Kansas City, Kansas. Thus we have two towns bearing the name of Kansas City, one in Missouri, the other in Kansas, both linked by a viaduct, and both enjoying the stench of the stockyards and packing plants, depending on whether the wind is blowing in from the east or from the west. Missourians, with characteristic pride, insist that when you say "Kansas City" you are speaking of the Missouri metropolis and not its Kansas satellite, for they point out that Kansas City, Kansas, is an appendage, an offshoot, a pretender, and, moreover, a place where all the pleasures of life are interdicted, including cigarettes and liquor. In this expression of self-conscious virility, pride, and contempt for competition from any source whatsoever, you have the veritable key that unlocks the whole swashbuckling story of Kansas City.

In the early days Kansas City's more conservative neighbors thought that this brash, "wide open" town with its gambling gentry and its real estate speculators would come to no good. The *Leavenworth Commercial* editorialized in 1872 about that "blustering, impotent Sodom at the mouth of the Kaw."

Kansas City's growth was phenomenal once the railroad bridge was thrown across the Missouri River. It soon overtook Independence, Lexington, Liberty and St. Joseph, in Missouri, and Leavenworth and Atchison, in Kansas—towns that at one time had brighter prospects than Kansas City. Today, with over half a million population, Kansas City is so far in front of the towns mentioned as to render any comparison ridiculous. Independence, once the bustling terminus of the Santa Fe Trail and a center of Mormon activity, is now a quiet suburb of Kansas City. The fact that it is President Truman's home town has brought it into the news, but even a President cannot recapture for Independence the glory that passed with the Santa Fe Trail. Lexington sleeps on its hill, proud of the cannonball half buried in one of the stone columns of its ancient courthouse a relic of the Civil War. Leavenworth, once a great supply depot, is now known for its Federal Penitentiary and its lovely old Army post.

BROTHER JIM AND THE WEST BOTTOMS

IT IS well to bear in mind that James Pendergast was a political boss in Kansas City long before his younger brother Tom came to power. Many people have forgotten this. Tom Pendergast's notorious career, ending in a widely-publicized trial, somewhat overshadows the life of his elder brother, who died in 1911. James, or Jim as everyone called him, achieved immortality in a statue in Kansas City's Mulkey Square, which is more than Tom ever achieved.

Jim came to Kansas City from St. Joseph in 1876, the year of the World's Fair in Philadelphia, which celebrated the Centennial of American Independence. Our country was still young, particularly the Midwest, and Jim Pendergast was younger still. He had just turned twenty and was already sprouting a mustache, obeying the dictates of the current fashion. It was the era of the mustache cup and the individual shaving mug in barber shops.

Jim got off the train at the depot in the West Bottoms. When he stepped outside and heard the rattle and clang of a busy industrial district, and got his first whiff of the West Bottoms air—a combination of smoke from switch engines, beer smells from damp saloons, packing plant exhalations, blacksmith shops, livery stables, river mud and stagnant swamp water—he knew he was in a man's world. When he strolled past the Blossom House and saw the tall cattlemen from the Southwest with their ten-gallon hats and cowboy boots standing in the lobby smoking fat cigars, and with gold and silver coins dangling from their watch chains, he knew he was going to like the place. As a matter of record it might be said that Jim Pendergast never outgrew the West Bottoms. They were his physical and spiritual home. He never left Kansas City from the day he got off the train until he died, except for brief visits to St. Joe and to Democratic conventions. When a convention delegation was being chosen Jim's name was one of the first to come up. He could be depended upon to hold the other delegates in line.

Upon his arrival in "Kaycee" or plain "K.C." as railroad men and hoboes affectionately nicknamed it, Jim promptly got a job as puddler in the A. J. Kelly Foundry, and later in the D. M. Jarboe Foundry. It was hard work and developed his muscles, which was no handicap in a tough ward where political differences were often settled with a straight right or an uppercut. In spite of his strength, soft-voiced and amiable Jim was not nearly as eager to use his fists as was his brother Tom. Legend says that Jim gave up drinking and fighting after a friendly tussle with one of his bosom friends, an encounter which rendered Jim's adversary *hors de combat*. It was one of those "I reckon I didn't know my own strength" sort of things.

In 1881, Jim Pendergast went into business for himself. He opened up an eating establishment and rooming house called the American House, on St. Louis Avenue. "Jim served some mighty fine meals," said Joe Shannon, a Pendergast political rival. In 1884, Jim opened up a saloon at St. Louis Avenue and Mulberry Street. He ran a "decent" bar and catered to railroad men. They trusted him and often turned their wages over to him for safe-keeping. Rough stuff was not permitted in Jim's saloon, and when young men drank too much he would load them in a buggy and drive them around to the neighborhood priest. He made them sign the pledge, and threatened to have nothing to do with them if they ever broke it. Like a great many other things Jim did, this was good political strategy. It won him the respect and votes of thankful parents. Later, at the crest of his political career, he remarked, "That's all there is to this 'boss' business—friends."

He got a taste of politics the very year he came to Kansas City. The Democrats threw a big picnic at the Fair Grounds to celebrate victories in Ohio and Indiana. A crowd of 25,000 turned out, and in no time at all consumed 17 oxen, 125 sheep, 40 hogs, dozens of chickens, several hogsheads of beer, and wagon loads of bread. Governor Charles H. Hardin was the main speaker. Jim learned his first valuable political lesson—free meals meant votes.

When Jim settled in the turbulent West Bottoms, Turner A. Gill was Mayor, and John Campbell and W. S. Gregory were Councilmen from the First Ward. In subsequent years Philip Casey, P. D. Etue, George W. McClelland, W. J. Ross, James M. Ford, Martin Regan, Patrick O'Rourke and James A. Finlay were Councilmen from the "Bloody First," and Jim knew them all. He worked hard at the polls, talked politics to his friends the railroad workers, did his quota of good deeds (helping the widows and orphans, feeding the down-and-outers, etc.). In 1892 he was persuaded to become a candidate for a seat on the City Council himself. In the First Ward he received 272 votes and his opponent received none! This was calculated to make a deep impression in political circles, and it did. Here was a vote-getter extraordinary. The slick politicians "up town" began to pay court to him. From 1892 to 1910 Jim Pendergast was never defeated at the polls. He never asked for any job more important than Councilman from the First Ward.

Reform movements hit Kansas City from time to time, and the temperance folk crusaded against saloons. Jim Pendergast, being a saloon owner, directed some caustic remarks in the direction of the reformers and the politicians who sought to curry favor with them. In 1888 the "barrel houses" on "Battle Row" on East Third Street were closed on Sundays for the first time in Kansas City's history. This was humiliating to a "wide open" town. Jim Pendergast was of the same stripe as the judge who reprimanded Carrie Nation. In 1901, Carrie Nation invaded Kansas City on one of her hatchet parties. She accused Kansas City of shipping "hell broth" over into Kansas. She was fined $5 and told to get out of town and go back to her native plains, since Kansas City, in the words of the judge, was "not a good place for short-haired women, long-haired men, and whistling girls." Carrie wore her hair bobbed, being a pioneer in this respect.

From year to year Jim Pendergast consolidated his political gains. He exerted influence far beyond that usually associated with the job of Councilman. Through his lieutenants he controlled a large block of votes, and could swing an election. People began to call him a "boss." The title was not misplaced, for the seat of political power and influence was not in the city hall but in the back room of Jim Pendergast's saloon. The following eulogistic account of Jim Pendergast is an illuminating document:

> "Politically, Mr. Pendergast's power and influence is much greater than any councilman's probably ever was. The undisputed leader of his own ward, he is also the acknowledged leader of at least half of the Democrats of Kansas City and Jackson County . . . His place * is the resort of the most distinguished men in the party and he is courted and flattered enough to turn the head of any man of less rugged sense. Jim Pendergast—as his friends call him—is a masterly organizer, a keen judge of men, a true friend and a generous foe. The secret of his political influence is found in none of these qualities, however, nor in the power of money, his own or corporate, which is commonly the case in the politics of

* Saloon at 510 Main Street.

> a great city. Neither does it rest in his big heart, and he has one of the biggest. His strength rests chiefly in the fact that he keeps his word and never breaks a promise. It is a common saying in Kansas City, 'Jim Pendergast's word is as good as his bond.' A rare virtue in any man, politician or otherwise." [1]

What a masterpiece of understatement! It seems to be the accepted rule to endow all bosses with a "big heart," a penchant for keeping all promises, and a word "as good as a bond."

THE APT APPRENTICE

BY 1890 James Pendergast was firmly entrenched in First Ward politics. And that year his younger brother, Tom, arrived in Kansas City.

It has often been said that Jim asked his younger brother to come to Kansas City to keep books for him. According to the standards of the time Tom had a fairly good education, for the Christian Brothers in St. Joseph put a good deal of emphasis on commercial subjects. This seems to jibe with Tom Pendergast's own version of why he came to Kansas City, as related to some of his old friends. We know that he had been a clerk for the Burlington Route. A railroad career did not appeal to him. Moreover, the railroads at that time were in bad repute throughout the Midwest. Their eloquent brochures had enticed thousands of land-hungry people to settle on farms which the railroads had obtained without cost

[1] *Political History of Jackson County,* Kansas City, 1902.

from the Government and which they in turn sold to the settlers on so-called easy-payment plans. Eastern bankers plastered the farms with mortgages. Grasshopper plagues, crop failures, and low prices for farm products brought on hard times, the mortgages fell due and could not be paid. Angry men and women poured out their wrath on the greedy railroads and upon Wall Street. In Kansas, Mary Elizabeth Lease, called the "Patrick Henry in petticoats," stormed up and down the country imploring farmers to "raise less corn and more hell," and wagons headed east bore the legend, "In God we trusted, in Kansas we busted." That the railroads deserved much of the censure heaped upon them is obvious to students of the period, and the lobbyists in Topeka, Kansas, and Jefferson City, Missouri, provoked considerable resentment with their bribes, their wholesale distribution of railroad passes to men they thought could help them put through legislation favorable to railroad interests, and their high-handed methods of getting what they wanted at any cost.

As a result of these abuses the Populists arose to form a new party. This was one of the most significant chapters in American history, and although the Populists were described by conservative elements in both major parties as a motley crowd of fanatics, the passage of time has shown them to be the true forerunners of many of the progressive movements of the past fifty years. Even William Allen White, who lambasted the Populists in his newspaper columns, confessed in his memoirs that he had been too harsh with them.

The Populist Revolt formed the background of Tom

Pendergast's entrance into Kansas City. The reforms advocated by this group of oppressed men and women left Pendergast unmoved. He hated reformers, hated them all his life, as a matter of fact. A New York *Times* reporter once described Tom Pendergast in these words: "He was a back-slapping, two-fisted, hard-cussing, bald-headed Missourian, an unreconstructed Democrat, who had only two hates—'those blank, blank, blank so and so Republicans and those blank, blank blue-nosed reformers.'"

When Thomas Joseph Pendergast arrived in Kansas City he took up residence with his brothers and sisters on St. Louis Avenue, in the West Bottoms. This unattractive section was in the First Ward. That it deserved the adjective "disreputable," applied to it by the aristocrats of "Quality Hill," is borne out by the *Census Reports* of 1890, the very year Tom Pendergast came to Kansas City. "From Mulberry Street east to the ward line was a low class of negroes. Along the river, west of Mulberry Street, were large slaughter and packing houses, fertilizing works, and railroad depots and yards. On both sides of Ninth Street were junk shops and secondhand clothing stores. In other portions of the ward the residents were chiefly Irish, German and native laborers." The high incidence of "gunshot wounds," as reported by the *Census,* reflected certain homicidal tendencies. It was that kind of a place. In later years, when Pendergast had a home in a swanky section of Kansas City's Country Club district, he threw a veil of silence over his early experiences in the West Bottoms. Culturally, it was on the wrong side of the tracks.

Jim Pendergast, with a diamond in his shirt, tipped his hat to the women of Mulberry Street, nodded to ragamuffins, and called all the railroad men by their first names. The West Bottoms represented his political empire. He soon started teaching his younger brother Tom the art and science of ward politics. Ringing doorbells, doing favors, passing out free meals, putting a scuttle of coal in front of someone's doorstep in the heart of winter, "fixing" things with the neighborhood "cop," helping the parish priest—all these things and many more were a part of the daily work. Where philanthropy ends and politics begins is a moot question. Tom Pendergast's own words are worth quoting: "I'm the boss. The reason I'm the boss is because of my ability. I know all the angles of organizing and every man I meet becomes my friend. I know how to select ward captains and I know how to get to the poor. Every one of my workers has a fund to buy food, coal, shoes and clothing. When a poor man comes to old Tom's boys for help we don't make one of those damn fool investigations like these city charities. No, by God, we fill his belly and warm his back and vote him our way." [1] Lincoln Steffens records a similar utterance from Martin Lomasney, boss of Ward Eight in Boston. "I think that there's got to be in every ward somebody that any bloke can come to—no matter what he's done—and get help. Help, you understand, none of your law and your justice, but help." These sentiments, so bluntly expressed, have the common touch. There is no getting around the fact that a successful political boss keeps close to the people he rules. It is a necessary part

[1] The New York *Times.* April 8, 1939.

of the game. Tom Pendergast got to know the common man pretty well when he worked in his brother's saloon. Some say he was a bartender. Others say he was a bouncer. Tom always denied that he was either. "I never sold as much as a glass of lemonade. I was a cashier." This seems likely, since another brother, John, was the regular bartender. Jim Pendergast brought several of his brothers and sisters to Kansas City around this time.

Jim, besides running a saloon, operated a concession at a race track. Old-timers say that Jim started in business for himself from winnings on a horse by the name of "Climax." Betting on the ponies was a family weakness, as later events were to prove. Speaking of his early days in Kansas City and the race track concession Tom Pendergast once told a group of his cronies: "I came to Kansas City when I was eighteen years of age. On arriving here I saw Jim and Jim asked me if I wanted a job and I told him I did, and he said, 'all right, go out to the race track and see Phil McCrory at the concession and tell him I want you to begin work.'" Pendergast turned to McCrory and said, "Phil, that was a long time ago, but I remember you were gray haired even then." [1] McCrory and Pendergast became business partners.

What was Tom Pendergast like at this period of his life? According to his intimates he was quite a "sport," a regular "rounder." He struck up an acquaintance with

[1] This information was given to me by one of Pendergast's friends who wishes to remain anonymous. For one thing it established the correct date of Pendergast's arrival in Kansas City. He was eighteen in 1890.

numerous landladies operating boarding houses. Like Jim, he wore a big black mustache, and he had an abundance of hair on his head with no indication of the baldness which was to come later. He was well put together, short, stocky, with a thick neck set on powerful shoulders. He stood 5 feet, 9 inches. He was full-faced, even then, and it was a manly face. He looked like an athlete, and he was one. His hands were very large and could grip a baseball bat firmly, but gracefully. He had the form of the born athlete. He was handy with his fists, and although he did not go out of his way to pick a fight he never as much as crossed a street to avoid one. He ran around with a bunch of Irish blades who could sing and fight with the best of them. Among his friends in the old days were Charlie Clarke, Mike Casey, Bert Brennon, and Mike Cunningham. Their favorite meeting place was Sullivan's saloon on the northwest corner of Missouri Avenue between 5th and 6th Streets. The opposition forces made Scanlan's saloon their headquarters.

These boys sang "Tim Toolan," "The Mulligan Guards," "In the Baggage Coach Ahead," "A Bird in a Gilded Cage," "She May Have Seen Better Days," and the current hit, "Ta-ra-ra Boom-de-ay." They went out to the ball park to watch the Kansas City Blues. On Sundays Tom attended Father Dalton's church in the West Bottoms. This Father Dalton was quite a character, and a scholar of some repute. He wrote about Kansas City's early history. The railroads ate into his parish, reducing it from one of the largest in Missouri to one of the smallest, but he labored on, for the West Bottoms was always, in the words of the old Negro spiritual, "standing in the need of prayer." Funerals were frequent, for besides the "gunshot wounds" previously mentioned these miasmic lowlands were plagued with the twin scourges of consumption and pneumonia.

I wish that Tom Pendergast had left a written account of these early days. He was anything but a literary man, and being a politician he knew that if he put anything in writing his words might trip him up. Fortunately for us another young man came to Kansas City the year after Pendergast arrived, and he had a great literary gift. The man I am referring to was William Allen White. In the warm glow of reminiscence White set down the following words: "The Kansas City of 1891, to which I came as Childe Roland to the Dark Tower, was an overgrown country town of a hundred thousand people. It was consciously citified, like a country jake in his first store clothes. It had one ten-story building, and a score of buildings from five to seven stories. Its business area comprised a dozen blocks in something like the center of town. To the west of the business area were the packing houses, which were inflated replicas of the stinking slaughterhouse in Eldorado. Around them were the small industries of the city and the stockyards, which smelled to high heaven. And of course fringing these were the shabby, unpainted homes of the workers. North of the business district was the red-light area, segregated and properly policed. South of the business area lived the ruling class in lovely homes surrounded by green lawns, with spreading elms, massive oaks, a few walnut trees, and young evergreens. There, in great ten-or-fifteen-room houses, surrounded by hundreds of feet of deep porches, in houses that bulged with the tumors and warts of the ornamental architecture of the jigsaw period, lived the bankers, the merchants, the lawyers, the doctors, the teachers, the preachers, now and then a prosperous gambler or a corrupt politician. These worthies were generally boycotted by the respectables, who were too nice to accept socially those whose business they tolerated, and whose immoralities were acknowledged as a part of the necessary social order of a boom town."[1]

I can attest to the accuracy of William Allen White's observations. His penetrating reference to the standing of corrupt politicians is exact. It is well to note that the Pendergasts did not create a political machine out of thin air. All the necessary parts were already there, waiting to be assembled.

It was around this time that "Pinky" Blitz and his gang were active. "Pinky" was a disgraceful commentary on civic virtue and provided a good target for William Rockhill Nelson's editorials in the *Star*. Nelson was a newcomer upon the scene, and he had a genius for getting under the community's skin. Frankly, he thought the people of Kansas City were uncivilized, and he wanted to introduce them to the finer things of life. He preached boulevards, parks, art galleries, theatres and operas. It disturbed him to know that men like "Pinky" Blitz were tolerated. He spoke of certain candidates for political office as "ignorant peddlers of whiskey."

A Nelson biographer, commenting upon the period,

[1] *The Autobiography of William Allen White*, New York, 1946. Copyright 1946 by the Macmillan Company, and used with their permission.

wrote, "Nowhere was electoral dishonesty and outrage more flagrant and obvious than in Kansas City in the years following the founding of the *Star*. These culminated in 1892-94 in a series of wholesale and daring frauds. Politics in both the county and city was dominated by a criminal gang, assured of immunity from punishment . . . Protected gambling was notorious . . . Elections were in charge of men who were absolute tools of the gang. False registrations were by thousands. Rowdies intimidated voters and kept them from the polls." [1] In 1894 twenty-one indictments for election fraud were handed down. Of the twenty-one indicted, twelve fled to parts unknown and one committed suicide. All of this will have a familiar ring before these pages are finished.

One can learn a lot about a city by reading through its *Code of Ordinances*. The politicians paid lip service to rules and regulations of a high moral tone. A certain Victorianism ran through the utterances of the City Fathers. It was unlawful for a prostitute to ride in an open carriage in Kansas City, and all girls who could not explain their presence on the streets after dark were looked upon as vagrants. "The playing of any musical instrument or instruments, or the making of any unusual noise or disturbance, or the singing by any person or persons, or the keeping of any parrot, quail, monkey, squirrel, or other bird or animal, in any saloon, or tippling house, or dramshop, is hereby prohibited." No one was allowed to carry a concealed pistol or revolver without permission of the mayor. Among the weapons prohibited

[1] *William Rockhill Nelson*. By members of the Staff of the Kansas City Star, Cambridge, 1915.

were, "any slung-shot, cross knuckles, knuckles of lead, brass or other metal, or any bowie knife, razor, billy, dirk, dirk-knife or dagger, or any knife resembling a bowie knife." Take the matter of licenses. An artist had to pay a fee of $10 a year, a corn doctor $10, a peddler of lightning rods $50, a photographer $50, a fortune teller $200, a keeper of a bucket shop $500, the keeper of a pool room $100. The license fee for a street exhibition was $10 a day, for a concert $10 a day, a cyclorama $100 per year, a panorama $100 a year, a theatrical exhibition $200 per year, a minstrel show $10 per day, a circus $250 for the first day, etc. Apparently the good people of Kansas City made no distinction between a corn doctor and a concert, a pool room and a panorama.

One of the early rackets was a bit of quackery known as lung testing. A yokel coming to Kansas City for the first time would be accosted by one of the fakirs. "Hey, Bud, how strong are your lungs? Want to have 'em tested?" Or he would be asked if he wanted to buy a muscle developer. So we find among the ordinances one requiring that "lung testers and muscle developers" be licensed.

When Tom Pendergast settled in Kansas City there was still a great deal of the spirit of the "Old South" in certain sections of town. Families loyal to the Confederacy were most likely to be found in the southern and eastern parts of the town. They still remembered that "Order Number Eleven," imposed by Union decree, forced them to abandon their homes in Jackson County and flee for their lives, nor did they forget the Battle of Westport, called "The Gettysburg of the West." The Union sympathizers, mostly transplanted New Englanders, clung, as if the name had something to do with it, to the northern sections of town. The more aristocratic segment of Union partisans withdrew to "Quality Hill," the last fortress of entrenched snobbery. The "Court House Crowd" of Jeffersonian Democrats coined the name "Quality Hill" to express their derision.

Kersey Coates, a Quaker from Pennsylvania, was the real founder of "Quality Hill." Colonel Coates built an opera house, one of the first in the West. (It burned down on the night of January 31, 1901.) He also built an imposing dwelling at the intersection of Lancaster (now West 10th Street) and Pennsylvania Avenue. The section known as "Quality Hill" covered an area about half a mile square. The families who lived there sent their sons to Andover and Yale, and their daughters to Wellesley and Smith. They sported fine carriages, employed liveried footmen. They set the tone. Today, "Quality Hill" exists only in a few decayed landmarks. "Quality" has migrated to the Country Club district and only the "Hill" remains.

To recapture some of the atmosphere of old Kansas City, and to get a better understanding of the early Pendergast era, I took a long walk on New Year's Day, 1947. I began at the north end where Jim and Tom Pendergast formerly dispensed hard liquor in Jim's levee saloons, then turned my steps toward Pennsylvania Avenue and "Quality Hill," a neighborhood that used to set its watches by the packing house whistle. A lot of ghosts walked with me—men of the bygone day in their Inverness capes and side-whiskers, the women with their wasp waists, leg-o-mutton sleeves, bustles, and trailing skirts that required yards and yards of expensive cloth. It was the golden age of the bicycle. Wheelmen were everywhere. Boys and girls rode tandem. I saw in memory the lamplighter, making his rounds with ladder and stick. Some of the ghosts had names. I recognized them as Tom Pendergast's "ghost votes" which I had seen so often on padded registration lists.

South of "Quality Hill" beyond Mulkey Square I came upon row after row of houses dating back to the 'Nineties and beyond, known in Pendergast's time as "Irish Hill." A little to the west on slightly lower terrain, and overlooking the West Bottoms, sat a figure in bronze on a marble base flanked on either side by a figure of a child. Engraved upon the statue were these words:

JAMES PENDERGAST
1856-1910 *
Alderman 1892-1910

There was an added inscription informing posterity that this statue was erected by contributions from the citizens of Kansas City. The statue has been mutilated by vandals time and again. The missing parts are replaced only to disappear. But Jim still gazes out across his beloved West Bottoms. I gazed at the bronze likeness of the saloon-keeper for a moment, turned up my coat collar to ward off the chill wind blowing out across Kersey Coates Drive, and walked on.

* I cannot account for this, since Jim Pendergast died in 1911.

THE INDUSTRIOUS JOURNEYMAN

A POLITICAL boss does not reach the top in one dramatic leap. He acquires his power gradually. He does not conquer a city in a sudden frontal attack. He takes it step by step while the people sleep. The annals of bossism will show that most political tyrants associated themselves with the city they were to rule before they reached the age of twenty-one. Jim Pendergast was twenty when he came to Kansas City, and Tom Pendergast was eighteen, as I have mentioned elsewhere. They followed the traditional pattern. Each began at the bottom of the ladder, first as a helper to a precinct captain, then by degrees rose to the leadership of a precinct, a ward, and then to the very top of the "organization," which is an accepted euphemism for political machine. Jim Pendergast started the "organization"—Tom Pendergast perfected it, adding a few new wrinkles of his own. The statue in Mulkey Square notwithstanding, everyone recognizes that Tom Pendergast was the political genius of the family. As John Gunther has recently pointed out, Jim was a "satrap of considerable eminence." But when he described Tom he said, "Boss Pendergast, the old man, is dead, but it is impossible to write about Missouri or indeed the United States without mentioning him." [1] I think that this is the commonly accepted view.

It was a foregone conclusion that Jim would pull a

[1] John Gunther, *Inside U.S.A.*, New York, Harper and Brothers, 1947. Copyright 1947 by Harper and Brothers and used with their permission.

few strings and get his younger brother a political job. Tom was an apt pupil, a good fighter, was popular with the "boys" who ran the city, had ambition. Jim confided to Tom that he was grooming him as his successor. The first political appointment came in 1896. County Marshal Chiles needed two deputy county marshals, and he appointed Tom J. Pendergast and Casimir John Joseph Michael Welch, or "Cas" Welch as it was much more convenient to call him. "Cas" had been secretary of the Local Plumbers' Union, and like Tom Pendergast was ambitious to be a "Big Shot" politician. The two men became friends, and in 1902 established the Hurry Messenger Service. Later, they became political rivals.

One of the leading Democrats of Kansas City at this time was James A. Reed. In 1900 he was elected Mayor. The Pendergasts attached themselves to Reed from the very start. Tom Pendergast idolized him. It was under Reed's administration that he got his first important post, Superintendent of Streets. A biographical compendium of this period describes Superintendent Pendergast as follows: "He has given his entire time and attention to the work, and his figure is a familiar one on the streets, standing in a snowstorm in winter, or in the broiling sun of summer, superintending the work of his men." [1]

It was on this job that Pendergast developed his abilities as a leader. He was the boss. He gave orders and expected them to be obeyed. If a worker got tough Tom boomed at him in his deep bass voice and brandished his powerful fists. Very few men wished to press the argu-

[1] *Political History of Kansas City.* Kansas City, 1902.

ment. It was around this time that Tom beat up a cop who was getting too rough with a young man Tom felt was being unduly persecuted. He was warned to leave the police department alone and to mind his own business. In other words he was told to stick to his street superintending.

Throughout his career Tom Pendergast followed the first rule of the jungle. He was a man of few words, and when those failed he used his big fists. He demanded loyalty from his followers. If someone got out of line or showed signs of insubordination, Tom called him into his office and in less time than it takes to read this sentence he knocked him down. He figured that this was the best way to handle ingrates. It was direct and it was convincing. Men were afraid of Pendergast, shrank from any physical encounter with him. How much this element of fear figured in the unchallenged and brutal progress of the Pendergast political machine is a matter no one has thoroughly explored, but I believe that it was an important factor, particularly since it spread its poison through a whole county. Pendergast used the evil arm of the underworld to spread terror when reform movements threatened to weaken his organization.

The year 1900 was a turning point in Tom Pendergast's career. That was the year of the Democratic National Convention in Kansas City, and the year Jim Pendergast and a handful of cronies founded the Jackson County Democratic Club. The date of the founding was August 29, 1900. A dozen Democrats met in the law office of L. B. Sawyer. A week later the permanent organization was set up at a big meeting held at the Midland

Hotel, a well appointed hostelry boasting the "finest and most expensive marble finishings of any hotel in America." This time 145 loyal Democrats were present, including Jim and Tom Pendergast. A club room was set up in the Navajo Building at 716 Delaware Street. It had billiard rooms, lunch rooms, bar, parlor and auditorium. A housewarming party was given on October 17, and about 3,000 Democrats turned out for what must have been a lively shindig. Membership reached 750 within a month. What was the purpose of this club? The announced objectives offer food for thought. It was organized "to promote harmony in the party, to put down factionalism in whatever way necessary, and to furnish a meeting place for good fellowship among Democrats of all shades of opinion." To put down the faction you did not happen to like by "whatever way necessary" appealed to a realistic boss like Jim Pendergast. The "boys" in the First Ward would have no difficulty in understanding such plain and pointed English. This was the club that became the Pendergast political machine.

The Democratic National Convention of 1900 brought Kansas City into national prominence. The enterprising spirit of the Midwest made a deep and lasting impression on the visiting delegates and newsmen. The Priests of Pallas had helped raise funds for a Convention Hall. The Flambeau Club had been organized in 1884, and out of this marching organization grew the Priests of Pallas in 1887. People like spectacles. They like mystery even more. Some mystical name had to be found for the commercial boosters. Delegations were sent to St. Louis and New Orleans to find out about the Veiled Prophets and the Mardi Gras. They came back with plans for a secret society, but they lacked a name. Someone suggested Priests of Pallas. It was adopted. The Carnival of September 14, 1887, was the first one given under the name of Priests of Pallas and 25,000 visitors came to see it.

As might be expected, the latter day followers of Pallas Athene were in the forefront of the agitation for a Convention Hall. One was built, and shortly thereafter, April 4, 1900, to be exact, it burned to the ground. The Democratic National Convention had already been scheduled for July. What was to be done? The prospect might have daunted most cities, but not Kansas City. Within ninety days a new Convention Hall arose. It was called the "Ninety Days Wonder." Hundreds of workmen worked night and day to achieve a miracle. They were still hammering away when the first delegates began to arrive. Eastern delegates shook their heads. The hall would never be ready in time. As a reporter for the *New York Daily Tribune* telegraphed to his editor on July 1, 1900: "Some fears are expressed by new arrivals regarding the possible failure to have the hall ready in time, but the genuine western push and energy characteristic of Kansas City encourages the belief that everything will be ready when Chairman Jones of the National Committee calls the Convention to order."

The same reporter remarked that David B. Hill, boss of upstate New York, had already arrived and had made a quick trip to Lincoln, Nebraska, to confer with William Jennings Bryan, and there was talk that he would most likely be the choice for Vice President. Everyone knew in advance that the "Boy Orator of the Platte" would be the nominee for President. The big fight would be over the nominee for his running mate. J. Hamilton Lewis, of Washington, he of the "auburn whiskers and flaming necktie" was on hand, and he made no bones about being a candidate. "For heaven's sakes, boys, keep people talking about me," he told reporters. The "Bryan and Sulzer Water Cocktail" suggested that Sulzer of New York might get the nod. Mayor Harrison of Chicago had a big following. He came with the eleven car special train from Chicago which bore the Cook County delegation, the Cook County Marching Club, three hundred strong, a brass band, and those two stalwart politicians, "Hinky Dink" Mike Kenna and "Bath House John" Coughlin.

The Montana millionaires, Marcus Daly and W. A. Clark, both claiming to have duly elected delegations, put up at the same hotel (The Midland) and both tossed off bottle after bottle of champagne at the bar. They scorned all other drinks. "Coin" Harvey, ex-Governor Altgeld of Illinois, Senator Teller of Colorado who had walked out on the Republican Convention because it would not adopt his free silver plank—these and hundreds of other notables jammed the hotels of Kansas City. Tom and Jim Pendergast were small fry in such an assemblage, but for the younger Pendergast it was an exciting, stimulating, never-to-be-forgotton spectacle. The Kansas City political machine seemed pretty small compared to "Big League" stuff like this. He watched the bosses in action. Being a pretty intelligent young man he made a lot of mental notes which were to come in handy later on.

He met, shook hands with, and exchanged pleasantries with a number of Tammany Hall delegates. Brother Jim was ubiquitous, dashing here and there, and extending Kansas City hospitality to many a visiting Irishman. The Tammany Hall delegation was almost solidly Irish. Senator Bernard F. Martin had been in charge of the nine car Tammany Hall special when it pulled out of New York. He had loaded the train with cases of liquor and tubs of Maine coast ice. "I don't want any good Tammany digestion ruined on this trip," he remarked. "Don't take any chances on that Missouri River water," he warned, "just stick to the case goods." Tammany boss Richard Croker was aboard, with Murphy and the other leaders. H. P. Belmont's private car, "The Mikado" was attached to the rear of the special train. The Tammany "Braves" made quite an impression on Tom Pendergast. The Midland Hotel rang with East Side slang, the Tammany delegates calling one another "Cull." Kansas City also made an impression on Tammany. The *Tribune* reporter, previously cited, wrote: "The Tammany men who are here are amazed at the way this city is 'wide open.' Nickel-in-the-slot gambling machines are to be found everywhere." Several such machines were in the Midland Hotel, and the delegates dropped nickels in them by the hour. The familiarity with which the westerners greeted strangers astonished the easterners. Judge Van Wyck, one of the more sedate Tammany delegates, was completely taken aback when a Kansas City man walked up to him with the greeting, "Van, old boy, how's your liver?" Judge Van Wyck replied: "I am very well, thank you," and after shaking the hand that was proffered him, turned and walked stiffly towards the billiard room of the Midland.

The Kansas City streets were filled with fakirs and button sellers. "Bim, the Button Man" was there. He had gambled on Bryan and Danforth being nominated and had a large quantity of buttons bearing their pictures. The Kansas City newspapers warned the delegates to be on guard against pickpockets and other underworld gentry and more or less guaranteed the presence of George Dickman, alias "The Squint," "Nosey" O'Brien, Charles Massamore alias "The Dice Box," "Baldy" Rice, "Old Bobby" Wright, "Black" Curtis, et al.

Considering the presence of Boss Croker, "Bath House" John, and David B. Hill, the following excerpt from the Kansas City *Times* is most illuminating: "The most conspicuous fact about the Kansas City convention as compared to that recently held in the City of Brotherly Love is that the Democratic assemblage is without a boss. It has been pointed out so emphatically that there can be no denial that the Philadelphia convention simply registered the will of the sleek, rotund Ohio boss, Mark Hanna. On the contrary, there are no bosses in evidence, none in hiding, and none expected in Kansas City." [1]

In spite of this, Boss Croker of Tammany Hall cracked the whip on David B. Hill. He publicly humiliated him and destroyed whatever chances he might have had to be Bryan's running mate. Tom Pendergast was fascinated with all this show of power. He learned that big conventions were often run from private suites in hotel rooms. He made up his mind that he would attend all subsequent national conventions, that he would some day have his

[1] *The Kansas City Times.* July 1, 1900.

own private car, and his own private rooms, and that he would pick his own delegates. History will bear witness to the gratification of all these ambitions.

Perhaps the great moment of the convention, as far as Pendergast was concerned, was the welcoming address of Mayor James A. Reed. Jim Reed, tall and slender, with the serious mien of a Roman Senator, stood before the vast audience that packed the hall, and his clear voice was heard in its farthest reaches. Reading that speech today one is impressed with its flowery rhetoric. It was a gem of its kind, and it brought down the house. He made Democracy sound so noble that men like the Pendergasts almost resolved to go straight. Fans rustled, coats were removed revealing pretty pink and fancy shirts. Delegates who had heard Bryan's "Cross of Gold" speech four years earlier were now being held spellbound by a man of almost equal powers of oratory. When Reed sat down, Tom Pendergast, Superintendent of Streets, arose with the rest of the crowd and joined in the demonstration. From that day on Tom Pendergast always kept a portrait of Jim Reed conspicuously displayed in his office.

III

PORTRAIT OF A BOSS

Goats and Rabbits

WHEN Jim Pendergast died in 1911, the newspapers said a lot of nice things about him. Kansas City had prospered in the time of his regime. When a city is growing, and a sufficient number of enterprising men make a lot of money, there is a marked reticence on their part to speak of corruption. A Chamber of Commerce dominated by these same men can cover up a multitude of civic sins, and the Kansas City Chamber was enthusiastic, articulate, boastful and blind. Its myopia was particularly acute when it came to discerning anything startling in the machinations of the Pendergasts. It was too busy creating slogans to see the handwriting on the wall.

As far back as 1889, Frank A. Faxon had coined the slogan, "Make Kansas City a Good Place to Live In," and this caught the fancy of "Baron" Nelson of the Kansas City *Star*. He made it a crusading motto. On the surface, Kansas City did become a good place in which to live. The magnificent acreage of Swope Park was thrown open to the public; J. C. Nichols, riding around the South Side in a buggy, saw the splendid possibilities of the area as a Country Club development; George E. Kessler, architect of the St. Louis World's Fair, was called to Kansas City with instructions to lift its face. When he arrived at the Union Depot and stepped outside he got a shock and also an idea. He looked at the shaggy bluffs covered with unpainted and dilapidated shacks and dozens of goats, quickly took out pencil and paper and started making rough sketches. From these sketches came the beautiful Kersey Coates Drive, Cliff Drive, and many other improvements which were adapted to Kansas City's unpromising terrain. Kessler spoke of the "topographical eccentricities" of the place, but he was a genius, and in a few years had given Kansas City its network of boulevards, which remain to this day. Like Nelson, he met with opposition on every side. The local residents scoffed at boulevards and parks, just as they scoffed at art. Miles Bulger, who will appear in these pages elsewhere, set the tone of the opposition with his famous remark, "I don't see no need of this. Art is on the bum in Kansas City."

Tom Pendergast was doing his part towards making Kansas City a good place to live in—a good place for Tom and his henchmen to live in. He was working as hard as Nelson, Kessler and Nichols, but in an entirely different direction. With brother Jim gone to his rest he was now in full command of the "organization." He was Superintendent of Streets again in 1908-1909 under Mayor Thomas T. Crittenden, Jr., and after Jim's death in 1911 became Councilman from the "Bloody First," serving in this post until 1916. After 1916 he refused to become a candidate for elective office. It cramped his style. He decided that he could exercise more power by pulling strings behind the scenes. With "stooges" in office he had more time to develop his talents as a boss. He wanted a free hand, and he got it, but he had to crack a few heads together in the process, and pull off a few big deals with rival Democrats who had their own aspirations to rule the local roost. With a man like Joe Shannon around, Pendergast's bid for leadership did not go unchallenged.

Shannon was the leader of the "Rabbit" faction of the Democratic organization, and Pendergast was the leader of the "Goat" faction of Kansas City and Jackson County Democrats. These odd terms will bear some explanation. In one of the hotly contested primaries a newsman referred to the fact that the Pendergast crowd "voted everything in sight, even the goats on the hillside," and another reporter countered with the remark that "the Shannon forces flocked to the polls like scared rabbits after the hunters had beaten the bush." These wisecracks served to brand the two factions as "Goats" and "Rabbits" from that time on. Another version is that the bluffs overlooking the West Bottoms, stronghold of Pendergast, were dotted with goats of poverty-stricken families, while the Shannon territory had once been filled with rabbits. Two or three other bizarre explanations have been given. How the terms gained currency is purely an academic question as far as I am concerned, and the reader is entitled to take his choice of origins. What I am more interested in is the manner in which the leader of each faction secured his dominant position in Missouri politics.

While the Pendergast dynasty was flourishing in the voting district known as the "Bloody First," where victory was always to the stout of heart and strong of fist, another son of Erin, the nimble-minded and suave Joseph B. Shannon, was coming rapidly to the front as a political rival. Like Tom Pendergast, he started at the bottom, and his career took him all the way to Washington, as Representative from the Fifth Congressional District of Missouri. In between was many a knock down and drag out battle with the Pendergasts, the victory going now to the one, then to the other. No holds were barred. No punches were pulled. It was one fighting Irishman against another. Kansas City was alternately amused and shocked by their antics. Since both belonged to the party of Jefferson and Jackson one might expect them to confine their attacks to the rival Republicans, who were always strong enough in Kansas City to offer a threat, and who were not without leaders, but no—they wielded the political shillalah on each other without stint, and set the tone for Kansas City politics.

Joseph B. Shannon was a picturesque figure. He was born in St. Louis in 1867. His father died when Joe was quite young, and the widow Shannon and her eight hungry children moved to the Ninth Ward in Kansas City in 1879. The Shannon home, despite straitened circumstances, was always filled with gay Irish laughter and many of the leading Democrats found a welcome there. Joe had to pick up odd jobs to help support the family, and this prevented him from getting an education. That he always had a thirst for knowledge is proved by the fact that he mastered the writings of Thomas Jefferson and became known in Congress as a Jeffersonian scholar. When his son was attending college Joe asked him to send home all the textbooks used in the courses he was pursuing. He read them carefully, took notes, and compared his notes with those of his son.

At one time in his youth Joe worked in Martin Keck's beer garden. His mother was horrified when she learned about it, and drew from him a promise never to touch a drop of liquor. Joe made the promise, and kept it—all his life. This sounds like the central figure in a Horatio Alger novel, and the comparison is not altogether out of line, but Shannon was no paragon of virtue when it came to crawling around in the mud and slime of Kansas City's ward politics. Fights with Jim and Tom Pendergast were not according to the Marquis of Queensberry rules. More often than not it was dog eat dog. As Pendergast and Shannon grew in power their feud grew more bitter. It was not uncommon to find one or the other making an alliance with the Republicans in order to defeat the candidates the rival faction had nominated in the primaries. This political chicanery brought on violent recriminations, but for one to charge the other with disloyalty was simply a case of "the pot calling the kettle black." No matter which side won, the people of Kansas City lost. Bossism was rotten no matter which way you looked at it, and it was only a question of whether the "Goats" or the "Rabbits" should take over City Hall. Sometimes the two factions met at the polls with sticks and stones and the air of Kansas City was rent with the sound and fury of a battle royal. The biggest, toughest, meanest looking "Goat" in town would lead the Pendergast contingent to the scene of battle, and the toughest, most durable "Rabbit" would head the Shannon forces. Spectators were always hoping to see the two champions come together for a fight to the finish. This was no War of the Roses. It was a backyard brawl that went on year after year.

Joe Shannon had started out as a friend of the Pendergasts. I have referred to the fact that Joe once praised the good meals Jim Pendergast served at the American House in the West Bottoms. Around the turn of the century the hot political question in Kansas City had to do with "Home Rule." Kansas City wanted to appoint its own police board instead of having the State of Missouri make the appointments. Shannon and his friend, Frank Walsh, were strong for "Home Rule." Other Democrats opposed it. Out of this came a party split which gave rise to the Jackson County Democratic Club in 1900. The Pendergasts could always be found on the side of Jim Reed. Reed and Walsh usually took opposite sides.

Joe Shannon and Jim Pendergast were drawn together on another occasion by virtue of their religious background. They fought the APA (American Protective Association) which was promoted largely by fanatics who openly preached intolerance and who were the Ku Klux Klansmen of their day. In 1894 Joe Shannon, Marcy K. Brown and Jim Pendergast helped defeat what was then known as the "Combine,"—Governor Francis and the City Hall group in Kansas City, and this victory allowed them to seize more power. They began to work out deals on a patronage basis, and after Jim's death Joe continued the same practice with Tom Pendergast, but he soon learned that Tom was a crafty customer and much more of a rival than the less subtle Jim. Between battles, and in spite of the fratricidal strife engendered by them, Tom and Joe remained personal friends. One of the odd features of American politics is the alacrity with which arch rivals in the primaries kiss and make up once the votes are counted. Shannon and Pendergast, jealous as they were of one another's increasing power, were smart enough to realize that it was better to divide the spoils than to have no spoils to divide. There was such a thing as carrying their rivalry too far, particularly since the hungry Republicans were sitting around like buzzards waiting to pick the bones of dead Democrats.

Joe Shannon was a versatile politician. He had spent several years in Jefferson City, Missouri, as an aide to Colonel William H. Phelps, the legislative lobbyist for the railroad interests. These years brought him in touch with the prominent statesmen of Missouri. He had a suave personality. He was a devoted disciple of William Joel Stone, former governor and later United States Senator from Missouri, and renowned as the most gifted of all Missouri politicians. Stone and Phelps, for many years close political friends, finally came to the parting of the ways, with Phelps declaring publicly that "both of us suck eggs but Stone hides the shells." In spite of this break, Shannon retained the friendship of both men, demonstrating his tact and diplomacy, a rare gift he employed to the day of his death. This caused one of his contemporaries to say, "Shannon can carry an armful of eels and never drop a one."

As a clever politician Shannon kept himself well informed as to what was going on. He was politically "the man about town." His headquarters were wherever he happened to be. This was in contrast with Tom Pendergast, who never moved from his headquarters at 1908 Main Street. He was unlike Pendergast in more ways than one. Whereas Pendergast lived a quiet life and retired at nine each evening, one might run into Shannon anywhere in the city talking to friends or foes at all hours of the night.

When aroused by some alleged disloyalty of a follower Shannon was a master of invective. I have heard him describe more than one man as a "clothes-line thief." Speaking of one of his erstwhile friends, he said to me, "Do you know that man was at one time a shoe salesman? Why, that fellow ruined the feet of half of the people of Kansas City." Apparently he was unable to recall any other misdeed of this delinquent. Shannon loved Democratic political conventions. He never missed one. However, if the Republicans held a convention in the Midwest he was just as likely to be found there, too, and he seemed to derive great pleasure from mingling with politicians.

Both Pendergast and Shannon were courted by candidates in other parts of the state, and their vote-getting proclivities in Jackson County were known to all politicians, but it cannot be said at this time that either one of them was strong enough to swing a statewide election. Their local feud sapped their strength. The battle for patronage finally ended in a truce. Pendergast and Shannon went into a huddle and came out with the announcement that henceforth they would divide patronage on a 50-50 basis. Certain city and county offices were by agreement allotted each faction and the patronage connected with each office was to be divided accordingly. This ended the rivalries in the primaries, and with the bosses in accord, factionalism, on the surface at least, seemed to have died down.

After battling Pendergast for years Shannon grew tired of being a local boss and decided to become a statesman. Pendergast's friends had no small part in bringing this about. They let it be known that Pendergast would throw the weight of his organization behind Shannon in order to send him to Congress. He was elected in 1930 and served in the House of Representatives until his death in 1943. With Shannon safely shelved in Washington, Pendergast became undisputed boss of Kansas City.

Shannon was a showman. In one of the Missouri congressional campaigns he hired a sound truck and some minstrels and toured the state with what to many people must have been more like a medicine show than anything else. But it won votes, and that was what Shannon figured it would do. This type of showmanship never appealed to Tom Pendergast. It was much easier to get votes by the simple expedient of padding the registration lists with names copied from tombstones and other ghostly records. Clubs, banquets and platforms held no attraction for Pendergast. He went out of his way to shun them. Pendergast understood human nature as well as Shannon but throughout his life he was jealous of his privacy. Certain secrets he kept to himself. Some of his closest friends never crossed the threshold of the Pendergast mansion on Ward Parkway. He never mixed his family life with politics.

In his last days Shannon was far removed from the local

issues that once agitated the ranks of the "Goats" and "Rabbits." He spent a great deal of his time sitting in the lobby of the Mayflower Hotel in Washington, D.C., surrounded by attentive cronies who were willing to listen to his long discourses on Thomas Jefferson and the sad state of government arising from ignorance of, or deviation from, true Jeffersonian doctrines. I recall a conversation I had with Shannon a few years ago. Without warning, and for no reason whatsoever, he suddenly launched into a long and vicious tirade against Mark Twain. He alleged that he had discovered Clemens had hired a substitute to fight for him during the Civil War. Thereafter, his speeches alternated between eulogies of Jefferson and damnation of Twain.

No account of Pendergast and Shannon would be complete without some reference to their satellites, Miles Bulger and Cas Welch. Bulger was a little man, aggressive and resourceful as very small men are likely to be, and he played the "Goats" against the "Rabbits." On some issues he was solidly behind Shannon, but for the most part he strung along with Pendergast. As a member of the city council he was regarded as a Pendergast henchman. When he achieved wealth and power he lived in a beautiful home on Ward Parkway, next door to Pendergast. At one time he conceived the idea of overthrowing Pendergast and becoming the boss himself. Pendergast could not believe the rumor at first, but when he found out that Miles Bulger had betrayed him he broke his power and cast him aside. It was like a bulldog tossing a Pekingese. Bulger, one bright summer day, was tripping lightly homeward when he espied his former friend Pendergast approaching in his limousine. When opposite him Miles turned facing him, and placing his thumb to his nose with his fingers extended, saluted the "boss." Pendergast applied the brakes, stopped his car, made a quick turn in the street and began chasing Bulger, whose speed was now something to marvel at. Bulger reached the door of his home just in time and thus escaped a good beating at the hands of his former friend.

One incident will suffice to reveal the character of Miles Bulger. I can vouch for it, for Miles told me about it himself. It happened during the days of Prohibition when the Federal Government was cracking down on moonshiners and dealers in the illicit liquor traffic. A friend and follower of his had been caught in the Federal dragnet and Miles called upon the U.S. District Judge in his chambers and related to him the fine qualities of his friend. Miles said he spread it on pretty thick, and it seemed to him the Judge was duly impressed by his plea until that jurist said, "Mr. Bulger, when this case comes up I want you to relate in court the story you have told me." Miles replied, "Hell, Judge, I'm not a lawyer; I'm just a fixer."

Cas Welch, like Bulger, had political ambitions. He was called the "Boss of 15th Street" and relished the title. The people of Kansas City named his crowd "Little Tammany." Like Bulger, he was a snappy dresser, and he was handy with his fists. He was always fighting someone on the slightest provocation. He had no formal education to speak of, but he read a little law on the side, enough to prove to his complete satisfaction that lawyers and law books were the real enemies of the people. As Justice of the Peace he scorned formal legal documents and drew up his own homely code. Disdain for the machinery of justice he carried to great lengths and many of his ignorant constituents regarded him as a sage and oracle. That he could make his own rules of court procedure in a city as large as Kansas City is a commentary on the political setup during the Pendergast era. Cas had a hankering for high society and he took up golf in order to hobnob with "gentlemen." He liked to be seen in fashionable places. He was Joe Shannon's lieutenant, but prided himself on having a certain autonomy in his own district, and in one of the Shannon-Pendergast patronage agreements he was able to horn in on 25% of the patronage. Pendergast did not take this threat of power seriously and was less concerned about Welch than he was about Bulger. Cas deserted Shannon in the 1924 campaign when the Ku Klux Klan was an issue and made peace with Pendergast. It may seem biologically impossible to turn a goat into a rabbit, but in Kansas City politics "Goats" often became "Rabbits" and vice versa. But the real goat was the long-suffering public.

WIDE OPEN

I RECALL the first time I ever saw Tom Pendergast. It was in 1911, shortly after his brother Jim passed away. He wore a black derby hat slightly cocked on one side of a massive head of bulldog proportions. His face was ruddy, and what impressed me most was his thick, bull-like neck that gave him the appearance of a wrestler. To me, as I look back, he was then the Pendergast in the "raw," long before the polish of his European travels had removed the rough edges. His voice was deep and throaty. I thought then, and I think now, that he was made to order for the pen of the cartoonist—a burly Irishman with a truculent look, an exaggerated paunch, and a big head crowned with a small derby. Nast's cartoons of Boss Tweed came to mind. Tweed weighed 300 pounds; Pendergast around 250 pounds.

Pendergast was not unmindful of the fact that he typified the boss. He derived a certain satisfaction from the fact that he was lampooned as such. It gave him a feeling of importance. He honestly believed that a political boss was an essential adjunct to Democracy. As he succinctly put it: "You've got to have boss leadership. Now look at me. I'm not bragging when I say I run the show in Kansas City. I am boss. If I was a Republican they would call me 'leader.' "

While Pendergast's political activities during the years constituted his main bid for fame, his business connections are not to be overlooked. His choice of investments indicated shrewd business acumen. Experience in his brother's saloon enabled him to establish his own liquor business. The T. J. Pendergast Wholesale Liquor Company made him a fortune, and still supports his family. He was one of the first to anticipate the coming of Prohibition. Year after year he had noted the gains of the W.T.C.U. with its white ribbons, parades and speeches. Only the ultra-wet votes of St. Louis had prevented Missouri from entering the "dry" column sooner than it did. Pendergast closed his liquor business when the Eighteenth Amendment was passed and waited patiently for its repeal. Meanwhile he turned to other forms of business for the revenue he needed. He established the Ready-Mixed Concrete Company and became its president. This was the first company to my knowledge to hit upon the happy idea of mixing concrete at the plant and then conveying it in trucks to the scene of construction. With the City Council and the County Courts under his thumb it was not difficult to obtain preferential treatment when it came to street and highway construction in Kansas City and Jackson County, and Pendergast's company enjoyed a virtual monopoly. Within a few years Pendergast owned the controlling interest in eight separate corporations. Each of these corporations was engaged in the manufacture and sale of various products needed by public services. His total income was enormous. Some of it was legitimate. Some of it did not bear the close scrutiny of agents from the U. S. Treasury Department. Yet, with a steady stream of money pouring into his strong box, his passion for betting on horse races brought him more than once to the brink of bankruptcy. He had to borrow from his business associates. This indulgence—it set him back well over a million dollars—earned for him the dubious distinction of being the biggest sucker in the realm of turfdom. Wagers amounting to $50,000 a day were not unusual when Pendergast was at the peak of his gambling mania. This penchant for the galloping ponies turned out to be his Achilles heel when I prepared the Government's case against him in 1938. More about that later.

Pendergast also dabbled in real estate. He became owner of the old Jefferson Hotel. Under his ownership this hostelry became the "night life" of Kansas City. "Night life" had always been considered a commercial asset to Kansas City due to the fact that hundreds of wealthy businessmen from the Southwest came there for entertainment. To them "K.C." was the only "recreational" center between the Mexican border and Chicago. After selling their steers in Kansas City's great stockyards, or their wheat in her capacious grain elevators, they were footloose and fancy free in a wide open town with plenty of "lettuce" in their bill-folds. Kansas City bawdy houses and gambling joints did a thriving business, and the burlesque shows were something *not* to write home about.

When the city's closing laws darkened the doors of other emporiums dispensing liquid refreshments the Jefferson Hotel went merrily on. There were no social barriers at the Jefferson. Its guests came from all walks of life. Gentlemen of the business world bored with mundane affairs sought solace in the spacious and ornate accommodations afforded by the Jefferson. There the *demimonde* of the city gathered nightly and cast amorous glances in the direction of anyone who seemed inclined to frivolity. The denizens of the underworld were not unwelcome as long as they did not display their wares in this social retreat. The management, in an effort to insure the safety of the patrons, thoughtfully provided two uniformed officers of the law.

In the basement of the Jefferson Hotel was one of Kansas City's earliest cabarets. Song writers tried out their new songs there, and one of the star performers was Tommy Lyman, credited with coining the phrase "torch song." Tommy went on to fame in New York and Paris.

Kansas City was one of the best burlesque and vaudeville towns in the country around this time. Joe Donegan ran the Century Burlesque Theatre. He also ran the Edward Hotel, and connected with it was the Edward Grill where show girls could come for a glass of beer and a bit of relaxation after their stage performances were over. Women were barred from saloons, so Donegan (called the "Angel of Twelfth Street") winked at the law a bit. Donegan put on such shows as "City Belles," "High Life Girls," "September Morning Glories," and "Zenola, the Girl with the Diamond Teeth." These were the days of Kathryn Durkin, the biggest drawing card Kansas City cabarets ever had. Billy Watson's "Beef Trust" and his "Krousemeyer's Alley" made a hit. Billy B. Van and the Beaumont Sisters were billed along with Eddie Foy, Valeska Surratt, and many other old favorites. There were several theatres operating: the Empress, run by Cy Jacobs; the Orpheum, managed by Martin Lehman; the Gayety, under Matt Smith; the Grand, under A. Judah; the Hippodrome, under Ben Starr. Stock companies visited the Auditorium. The Willis Wood Theatre, managed by Roy Crawford, was popular. The real hot spots, however, were the Century Theatre, the Jefferson Hotel cabaret and the Edward Grill.

I distinctly remember those days, for my home town of Richmond was less than forty miles from Kansas City. I made many a trip to the "Big City." Among the odds and ends of memories associated with "K.C." were the following: Electric Park with its myriads of electric bulbs, its roller coaster, Pryor's Band, and a dazzling, semi-nude woman rising out of the waters of the Electric Park pool with colored lights playing upon a fountain of cascading waters; Fairmount Park, featuring "A Night in Old Heidelberg"; Woolworth's Five and Ten on Main Street where the country girls crowded around the sheet music department to hear their favorite songs sung by a handsome singer who winked at them as he sang, causing many a female breast to flutter with excitement; the shows at the Gayety and the Hippodrome.

This was the beginning of the "Jazz Age." Pendergast indirectly had a great deal to do with it. The jazz artists flourished in "wide open" towns like New Orleans, Chicago and Kansas City. Under Pendergast everyone knew that the lid was off in Kansas City and band leaders, show folks and the gamblers who always show up where there is plenty of entertainment, flocked to Kansas City in droves, fleeing dull places not blessed with boss rule. Underworld characters picked Kansas City as their favorite rendezvous. During Prohibition the advantages of a place like Kansas City were obvious to all who were bent on breaking the laws. Give Tom Pendergast the full credit. His political machine provided the necessary protection through its links with the underworld.

The Jefferson Hotel went out when Prohibition came in. Pendergast sold this night spot in 1919 for around $80,000. The six-story brick hotel near Market Square was conveniently condemned to make way for the widening of a street, and Pendergast's friends saw to it that he was awarded more for the condemned edifice than he had asked for, so strong were their charitable impulses. It should be noted that Tom sold his hotel just in time. He had no desire to run a "speakeasy" or have his name connected with such a place. If his henchmen wanted to cut in on some of the profit the underworld derived from bootlegging that was their business. He simply got out of the liquor business and concentrated on making ready-mixed concrete. Tom knew what he was doing. He wanted to keep Government agents off his trail, and for very good reasons, as subsequent chapters will show.

In Kansas City a whole new school of jazz music was born. Bennie Moten, Count Basie, Walter "Hot Lips" Page, Andy Kirk and others kept the Reno Club and other hot spots jumping with rhythm. I am no authority on jazz, and must take the word of others about this phase of Kansas City's cultural renaissance. The only point I would like to make is that all this flourished during the Pendergast era and because of it. When the underworld flocks to Chicago, New Orleans, Miami and Kansas City it has to be entertained on a wild and lavish scale. It demands music, women and gambling tables, and while engaged in the pursuit of "high life" it wants protection from snoopers, reformers, and policemen who may be a bit overzealous in upholding the law. Under John Lazia and other Pendergast henchmen Kansas City provided this freedom from molestation. I cannot overemphasize this. It set the stage for such things as the vote fraud scandal, the Union Station Massacre, and other dark chapters in Kansas City's history.

This was Pendergast's Kansas City—with its "Walkathon" at El Torreon which lasted for 117 days, and its Chesterfield Club where the waitresses, as described by Westbrook Pegler, went from table to table wearing nothing but high-heeled slippers. Such bizarre citizens as gum-chewing John Lazia, slot machine king; Gold Tooth Maxie the crapshooter; gargantuan Solly Weissman the "fixer"; Hard Luck Charley Haughton, who was head man in the gambling colony; Verne Miller the bank robber—these were but a few of the men who made life interesting and dangerous in a city that called itself the "Heart of America" and adopted as its slogan, "Make Kansas City a Good Place to Live In."

THE FITNESS OF THINGS

AS THE years went by, and his prosperity mounted, there was a gradual but decided change in the Boss's way of life.

On January 25, 1911, in Belleville, Illinois, occurred a civil wedding which attracted little publicity at the time. Thomas J. Pendergast, 38, and Carrie Snider, 27, who gave their address as Kansas City, Missouri, were united in wedlock. It was the culmination of a long acquaintance. On the same day the Kansas City *Star* carried the headline: "IS T. J. PENDERGAST MARRIED?" Another line read: "The Alderman's Friends are not Certain it was He." The brief story went on to say that Alderman Pendergast had gone on a business trip to Cincinnati. Relatives and friends said they had no hint he contemplated matrimony. The name Carrie Snider was unfamiliar to them. Two days later the *Star* ran these heads: "IT'S TRUE, PENDERGAST SAYS. The Alderman's Little Elopement was to Avoid Publicity." The *Star* added: "Alderman Thomas J. Pendergast returned home this morning from an eastern trip, and confirmed the report that he married Miss Carrie Snider Wednesday morning in Belleville, Ill. She had been living in Los Angeles for some time but formerly lived here. The marriage was the result of a long standing engagement. They went to Belleville to avoid publicity."

Seven days after the civil ceremony Pendergast and his bride were married a second time in Kansas City, but on this occasion the ceremony was in accordance with the rites of the Catholic Church. Once again no publicity was given the marriage in deference to the personal wishes of the boss. For the rest of his life he drew a veil of silence over his domestic affairs. He demanded privacy and got it. Few of his friends ever entered his home. If they wanted to see him they could call at his office at 1908 Main Street or could chat with him at the race track or at a political gathering. In later years, he took his wife and children to New York and Saratoga, to Colorado Springs and other pleasure spots, and the sleek and high-powered roadsters his wife and daughter drove were known to residents of the Country Club district, but the mansion on Ward Parkway bore an air of privacy that few people were able to penetrate.

I have just spoken of the Pendergast home on Ward Parkway. It was a far cry from the humble room over Jim Pendergast's saloon in the West Bottoms where Tom had spent his first weeks in Kansas City. I quote from the *Star*: "Gradually there is taking form at 5650 Ward Parkway a house whose precision and symmetry of line suggests an architectural influence not often encountered in Kansas City, the classic manner of the French Regency.

The house is the architectural work of Ed. W. Tanner, head of the J. C. Nichols Company's department of design. It will be occupied and owned by Mr. and Mrs. T. J. Pendergast, who have lived for some years at 54th and Wyandotte Street. It was coincident with the building of the Wyandotte Street house that the Democratic leader left the city council."

The spacious hall was described, along with the wrought-iron stairs, walls paneled in French style, and other details. "The combination of rosehued bricks, laid in white mortar, with softshaded slate, makes the few exterior decorations stand out prominently. The massive wrought-iron door with its vertical panes of glass, the cut stone cornucopia placed above the stone frame that encloses it, and the three sturdy chimneys attract the eye of the beholder."

The inside of the house was expensively furnished, matching and surpassing the elegance of the exterior. Neither Tom nor his wife did much of the planning. Everything was left to the judgment of interior decorators. A French note prevailed, with all the gilt and glitter of the Louis XV period. The whole downstairs was carpeted from wall to wall. "You got the impression of sinking into those carpets up to your knees," remarked one visitor. The wood paneling was perfect in every respect and very French, and delicate chairs and other objects occupied just the right spot in the right room. That the ex-saloonkeeper ever felt at home in this house is extremely doubtful. He had a habit of retiring to his own room at an early hour, usually around nine o'clock, and he tolerated no noisy parties. His room, like all the other bedrooms, was done in color. If the walls were pink the bed coverings were pink—even the sheets were pink, and if the walls were blue all the bed furnishings were blue. Closets bulged with expensive shoes, hats, furs, etc.

In the basement was a recreation room with a completely stocked bar across one whole side. A nautical motif prevailed—anchors and lifebuoys and all that sort of thing. In Kansas City this seemed inappropriate. Leather and chromium bar stools were provided for the guests. The bar itself was one that Pendergast saw in New York, liked, and purchased on the spot. He spent very little time in it, for in his later years he seldom if ever took a drink. Perhaps the expression that best sums up the whole interior of the Pendergast mansion is "nouveau riche."

In 1929, Pendergast fell victim to the very scum his benevolence had entrenched in Kansas City's underworld. His mansion was robbed! The Kansas City *Times*, September 4, 1929, reported the robbery as follows: "The home of T. J. Pendergast, Democratic organization leader, was robbed last night of jewelry and clothing, valued from $100,000 to $150,000. Much of the lost was rare jewelry and fur pieces, including the engagement ring of Miss Marceline Pendergast, who is to be wed October 15. Part of her trousseau was also taken including 40 doz. pairs of silk hose. The baffling robbery occurred while four children played in the basement playroom of the big new home at 5650 Ward Parkway and while a maid slept on the third floor.

"The robbers worked on the second floor, looting seven rooms there. Many of the most valuable pieces of jewelry were gifts to Mrs. Pendergast. . . . Mrs. Pendergast estimated the value of the jewelry alone at $150,000.00. . . . Members of the Pendergast family returned only yesterday morning from New York where they were attending the races and shopping for Miss Marceline's trousseau. They were called home by the death of Mr. Pendergast's brother, Michael.

"Last night at 8:00, Mr. and Mrs. Pendergast went to the M. J. Pendergast home to attend the wake. They returned at 11:00 to find the second floor looted.

"Mrs. Pendergast had carried her jewelry from New York in a chamois handbag. The jewels, mostly diamonds, some of the pieces being rare specimens, were wrapped carefully in tissue paper. Because of the excitement of her return yesterday, Mrs. Pendergast did not place the jewels in a safe deposit vault, as was her custom. She left them in the bag and last night hid the bag behind a dressing table. The burglars found it and took the valuable pieces. From a closet they took a rare Manchurian fur coat, valued at $1,375.00, and three fox furs, valued at $1,200.00.

"Dozens of gifts including several jeweled cigarette lighters purchased as gifts for the wedding, were taken, also two valuable cigarette lighters with watches encased, belonging to Mr. Pendergast. A roll of about $3,000.00 which Mr. Pendergast had put under a mattress of a bed in his sleeping room, the same room where Mrs. Pendergast hid her bag was not touched. Mrs. Pendergast was inclined to believe a woman had a hand in the robbery, as the robbers took only fur pieces of latest fashion."

Tom Pendergast offered a $10,000 reward for the return of the stolen property. The jewels were insured for $6,000, part of a $10,000 insurance policy including household objects. Pendergast thought that the robbers were Kansas City men.

At this particular moment Pendergast was doing very nicely for himself financially. His chief source of income was from the Ready-Mixed Concrete Company. A great many people knew that Pendergast had a monopoly in concrete, but few had the courage to say so. Kansas Citians were therefore somewhat surprised to read in the *Star*, September 8, 1928:

"BEACH OPENS UP
Ready Mixed Concrete and Pendergast Robbery
are Targets for Mayor's Sarcasm"

The article began: "Mayor Beach last night rolled the city's spring campaign off to an early start. The Ready-Mixed concrete business of Tom Pendergast, Democratic boss, failure of the Democratic administration and the recent $150,000 robbery at the Pendergast home were among the subjects dealt with by the Mayor . . . The Mayor's talk bristled with challenges and no small amount of sarcasm . . . 'The time has come for the Republicans to play smart politics. Forget differences and jealousies and put up a ticket that will win,' he said. 'For the first time in the history of the city a boss has put his name on wagons and flaunted it over the city,' the Mayor stated, referring to Pendergast and the Ready-Mixed concrete.

"Mayor Beach asserted specifications in the public works department had been so prepared in regard to machinery for the mixing of concrete that contractors have little choice except ready-mixed. He further cited what he termed a story heard in regard to a certain big building where there was a refusal at first to buy Ready-Mixed concrete, but where it was finally used. The Mayor related the builder was forced to tear out footings installed after he was called upon and instructed to remove the work because it was charged it had been damaged by 'frost.' 'The result was the builder bought Ready-Mixed,' said the Mayor.

"Go out on Ward Parkway and there you will see the wonderful mansion of T. J. Pendergast—said to have cost $100,000 with furnishings costing $75,000. The other night a thief stole into the master's bedroom. Among the jewelry taken was a 6-inch bar pin worth $10,000. That is more than my home cost,' added the Mayor as he read to the audience from the list of jewelry stolen. 'And several fur coats and overlooked four! Forty dozen pr. of silk hose—that is 480 pair, enough to stocking all the women in this crowd for a year! And rumor has it that Tom's silk underwear was taken. My friends, the Republican party is no longer the silk stocking party. The Democratic party now is.'"

The Mayor's outburst came like a bombshell. People in high places did not talk about Boss Pendergast that way. At the next Council meeting the Democrats turned their verbal fire on the Mayor. The meeting began with the reading of a communication from City Manager McElroy which quoted the Mayor's recent speech, and which requested him to name the builder, the location, and all other facts he had relative to the alleged forced use of Ready-Mixed concrete so that the Council could start an investigation. Councilman A. N. Gossett, Democrat, called upon any citizen who had evidence of coercion upon the part of Pendergast's company to furnish the Council with such evidence. The Mayor replied that the information used in his speech had been given him in confidence.

The arguments waxed hot, and a lot of charges were made. Some wanted to call a Grand Jury investigation. Others accused Mayor Beach of being a coward for not divulging the source of his information. City Manager McElroy had more power and influence than the Mayor, since he was known to be friendly to the Pendergast cause. In fact, he took orders from Pendergast; had been under obligation to him since 1922, the year the "Boss" had raised him to a judgeship of the County Court.

Pendergast was not greatly disturbed by what Mayor Beach had to say. He knew that McElroy was in the driver's seat. He himself was so securely entrenched in power that he could make trips to Europe with never a worry about being overthrown in *absentia*. On July 11, 1927, Pendergast, on stationery of the Hotel de L'Univers, Tours, France, had written to the "boys" of the Jackson County Democratic Club: "As it is impossible to write to all members, I am taking this means of letting you know that I think of all at some time or other on my trip, and I can truthfully subscribe to the old adage, 'Distance makes the heart grow fonder.' My family and I are having a wonderful time. We have enjoyed best of health and have toured England, Ireland, Scotland, and Wales, and found the rural parts very lovely—the cities not so good, except London which is very large and very busy—traffic about as congested as New York, but not so well regulated. We flew to Paris from London. I do not think I would do it again. The noise from the engines was deafening, and our ears rang for 24 hours afterward. Paris is truly a wonder city. We spent 8 days there, and were treated with every consideration. I found no evidence of bitterness or price gouging."

THE KNOW-HOW

TWO events, one local and the other statewide, paved the way for the consolidation of Pendergast's power. He was strong before they took place, but after they went into effect he was a dictator in the full sense of that term. The first was the new Kansas City charter, voted into existence in 1925, the other the redistricting of congressional districts in 1931. The charter was designed to check the corrupt and greedy ambitions of Pendergast and his organization. It seemed enlightened and progressive. "Big Tom" watched these developments out of the corner of his eye. He called in his legal "brains" for a conference. He outlined his strategy. He examined the loopholes. He let it be known before the election that he was all in favor of the charter. It would provide for a City Manager form of government. Fine! He had no objections to a City Manager. Could this be Pendergast speaking? The people of Kansas City rubbed their eyes in amazement. Did he know he was licked? Was he preparing to step out of the picture? They did not have to wait long for an answer, but the answer was not the one they dared hope for as they went to the polls February 24, 1925, and strongly endorsed the new charter and the

City Manager form of government. The new plan became effective April 10, 1926.

"On the fourth day after the election (following adoption of charter) a meeting of the leaders of the Democratic organization was called by the Democratic campaign chairman for the purpose of discussing the selection of a City Manager. This meeting was attended by T. J. Pendergast . . . at a caucus of the Democratic members-elect of the City Council the choice of H. F. McElroy was affirmed . . . The Republican members of the council-elect were not consulted in the selection. The partisan character of the first administration was soon plainly evident—He (McElroy) appointed as department heads only well recognized Democrats, all but two of whom, like himself, were members of the Pendergast or 'Goat' faction."[1] In less than six months after the adoption of the charter nearly half of the city's former employees were dropped from the payrolls and loyal Pendergast henchmen replaced them. Pendergast had taken over the city in a brash coup that stunned and humiliated the voters of Kansas City.

An honest, fearless City Manager determined to carry out the provisions of the new charter could have dealt a death blow to the Pendergast machine. The provisions under the section devoted to "personnel" would have taken care of that, but of all the provisions in the new charter the ones on personnel were the ones most brazenly flaunted. The success or failure of the City Manager form of government depended on the character and

[1] Henry M. Alexander: The City Manager Plan in Kansas City. *Missouri Historical Review*, January, 1940.

ability of the City Manager and the character of a small, stream-lined City Council. McElroy was a Pendergast tool, and the majority of the members of the City Council were under obligation to the boss and could be depended on to vote the way he wanted them to vote. Instead of freedom the people of Kansas City had unwittingly voted themselves into a strait-jacket. They were worse off than they were before. The Mayor became a figurehead, someone to throw out the first ball at a baseball inaugural or to greet visiting Chamber of Commerce delegations—the real power was in the hands of the City Manager, or, as more and more incidents were to prove, in the hands of Pendergast.

Let us take a look at this City Manager. Henry F. McElroy grew up in Dunlap, Iowa. As a boy he dabbled in small business undertakings and made more money than the average person his age, chiefly because he had devised his own system of bookkeeping. He developed some short cuts, and evolved a few economic theories of his own. They may or may not have been unscrupulous, but they were at least highly unorthodox. He had very little schooling. With his native ability and shrewdness he had little use for formal education. He knew that he could always "get by" and he was determined to grab the main chance the moment opportunity knocked. He moved to Kansas City and got a job. Later he made a fortune in the bakery business. Nothing startling happened until 1922. In that year Pendergast wanted to give Miles Bulger a sound licking. Miles was then a judge of the County Court, and Pendergast wanted to blast him off. Pendergast put Harry S. Truman and Henry F. McElroy in the race for two of the judgeships and both won.

McElroy carried his unorthodox bookkeeping theories into the City Manager's office. He had novel ways of balancing the budget. He robbed Peter to pay Paul. By neat juggling he was able to transfer funds from one department to another. Deficits simply disappeared as if by magic. Sound economists knew that no generally accepted methods of doing business could produce the figures blandly tossed around by the mathematical genius in City Hall. They challenged his figures. He dismissed them with a wave of the hand or confused them with "double talk." Kansas City was booming. Look at the new streets, the new buildings, the great airport, one of the finest in the world. Unemployment? Depression? Kansas City, far from being licked by the world-wide depression, was actually going forward. She had her "Ten Year Plan." McElroy, as much as any other official in America, created the fine art of "boondoggling." Harmless Brush Creek, a trickling brook meandering peacefully through a swanky residential section of Kansas City, was paved—widened and paved as though it were a traffic artery—and with Pendergast's Ready-Mixed concrete to be sure! The pick and shovel brigades of Henry F. McElroy, the speech-making and organizational efforts of Conrad H. Mann,*

* Mann was a Republican, but he often played ball with Tom Pendergast. The Eagles moved their national headquarters to Kansas City in 1907, with Mann in charge. He soon became the spark plug of the Chamber of Commerce. In 1932 he was convicted on a charge of violating the lottery laws. He staged an Eagle frolic and took in over a million dollars. It was alleged that he took a cut in this. Tom Pendergast went to Washington to get President Roosevelt to pardon Mann, but F.D.R. refused to see him. Tom then went to Jim Farley. All appeals failed.

head of the Kansas City Chamber of Commerce and leader of the Eagles, the Committee of 1000, and the lavish Federal aid dispensed by the New Deal gave Kansas City a public building program of enormous proportions. These public improvements cost around $50,000,000. It was not until Pendergast and McElroy were caught in the clutches of the law that the people of Kansas City discovered the shocking state of its financial affairs.

McElroy's regime was never a bed of roses. He had a fist fight with Miles Bulger. He tangled with Rabbi Mayerberg, a reforming zealot who fearlessly attacked the Pendergast machine, and who demanded to see some of the city records. He walked into McElroy's office, read off a list of charges of civic corruption and asked the City Manager point blank to explain some of his fancy bookkeeping. McElroy rudely rebuffed him. As he left the office Rabbi Mayerberg encountered John Lazia, kingpin of the underworld and one of Pendergast's lieutenants. "You didn't get very far, did you?" he said to the indignant Rabbi in a taunting manner. It soon became necessary for Rabbi Mayerberg to travel around the city in a bullet-proof automobile.

I think that I have revealed enough facts to show that the new charter of 1925 played into Pendergast's hands. Now a word or two about the second factor that made Pendergast supreme commander of Missouri politics. The redistricting act was passed in 1931. It provided for 13 Congressional districts instead of 15, a reduction made necessary by a drop in population. An area covered in a Congressional district was based on the population of that area. To the surprise of almost everyone the Governor of Missouri vetoed the act. This meant that the next candidates for Congress would have to be elected at large. Instead of voting for the candidate from one district the voters were required to vote for the candidates from all the districts. How did this help Pendergast? The answer is simple: Pendergast's Kansas City and Jackson County machine controlled such a large segment of the State's voting strength that it was almost impossible for a candidate running at large to be elected without the support of this machine. Consequently, a great many candidates from other parts of the State had to make a courtesy call to Pendergast's office at 1908 Main Street and beg for his support. Pendergast's backing was tantamount to election, his disapproval meant almost certain defeat. Some candidates refused to make such a groveling gesture to the boss, but many made the pilgrimage to 1908 Main Street. This gave the tyrant an inflated sense of importance. He could call the turn, and the experience went to his head. Prior to 1931 he was undisputed boss of Kansas City. Now he was undisputed boss of the State of Missouri. He dominated the State Legislature. The Capitol Building at Jefferson City was called "Uncle Tom's Cabin." His influence reached all the way to Washington, D.C. Overnight he had become a national leader, and men like Jim Farley paid open court to him. If he could swing Missouri in a closely contested national election his friendship was well worth cultivating.

In his first test of strength under the new dispensation Pendergast elected the Governor of Missouri, most of the State officers, a big percentage of the thirteen congressional candidates backed by the machine, but his choice for U.S. Senator was defeated by Bennett C. Clark, son of Champ Clark, illustrious Speaker of the House of Representatives who barely missed being President of the United States in 1912. Champ Clark had been a hero in Missouri, and will always be associated with the song, "You've gotta quit kickin' my dawg around." I can never forget old Champ. In the twilight of his career, tall and gaunt and gray, with the simple dignity and wisdom of an elder statesman, he came to Ray County to make a speech in behalf of my younger brother, just back from the First World War and at that time running for a pivotal seat in the National House of Representatives. The son of a man of this stature was assured of a big following to start with. Moreover, Bennett C. Clark had a creditable war record, was one of the original founders of the American Legion in the Paris Caucus of March, 1919, and he was campaigning openly for the repeal of Prohibition. This combination of factors more than offset the Pendergast power, but it was an isolated instance.

Clark, backed by the "wet" vote of St. Louis, won the race. Such a victory was understandable. Few looked upon it as a personal defeat for the boss. Pendergast's candidate for the governorship, Francis M. Wilson, was nominated by an overwhelming vote, but died suddenly, just before the November election, leaving a most important vacancy in the Democratic State ticket.

Wilson's death was a shock to Missouri Democrats, indeed, a paralyzing blow. Did this daunt Pendergast? Not in the least. He simply selected another man to carry on the fight, a fellow townsman of the deceased, a circuit judge by the name of Guy B. Park. Pendergast convinced the State Democratic Committee of the wisdom of his choice, and the hastily selected substitute candidate was elected Governor of Missouri. The brilliant strategy of this move established Pendergast as "dictator" of Missouri politics for the next eight years. The key appointments in the State administration, with very few exceptions, bore the Pendergast stamp. The editors of the *St. Louis Post-Dispatch,* bemoaning the lack of civic spunk in the sister city to the west, cried "Shame! Shame!" Fitzpatrick's cartoons hit home, but Pendergast's acknowledged power removed the sting of editorial criticism.

It was in 1932 that Pendergast and his crowd made their famous junket to St. Louis, taking that city by storm. "The Boys Put It Over," read the headline of the *Kansas City Times,* March 29, 1932, describing the exodus of 5,000 Pendergast precinct pollers from stunned St. Louis. "There is no doubt now," the article said, "that Pendergast has been accorded by St. Louis his place as a leader. All St. Louis newspapers published his picture, and used words which usually are associated with political bosses, telling how 'the Kansas City boss makes his slate,' and 'Tom Pendergast dominates the convention.' Followers of the Kansas City organization leader look at the headlines and pictures of their boss and smile. That's the kind of a boss they like, so they say—an easy winner. The Kansas Citians missed very little at the convention. They could tell exactly where Pendergast was standing when the big Jackson County block of votes was announced, yes—the 'boss' was smiling and wasn't that smile on the boss's face worth seeing? It was a worn out crowd of men and women which returned to Kansas City at last on three special trains, from the big Democratic demonstration in St. Louis. Among those on the trains were Judge Harry S. Truman of the County Court; E. Mayorie Melton; Otto C. Murphy, Chief of Health Inspection for the city; Emmett A. Scanlan, Chief Fire Inspector; Joseph Overly, Dem. leader in the east bottoms; James Gilmer, Marriage License Clerk.

"A large North Side delegation, headed by John Lazia, entered the station shortly before 11 o'clock."

At the very crest of his power Pendergast was interviewed by Ralph Coghlan, an editorial writer for the *St. Louis Post-Dispatch.* Coghlan visited the boss at his office at 1908 Main Street. The story appeared in *Forum and Century,* February, 1937.

Here are a few excerpts: "Mr. Pendergast, you are a great power in this state. You were recently called in The New York *Times,* in an article written by its Washington correspondent, Arthur Krock, the most powerful boss in America and one of the most interesting citizens of America."

"Well!"

"We want to know something about you, about your philosophy, if not of life, of politics. You are a realist, are you not?"

"What do you mean?"

"You take a practical view of things?"

"That's me."

Here followed a lengthy series of questions and answers in regard to how a political machine functions, does favors, gets out the vote. Coghlan then queried: "When you endorse a man for office, Mr. Pendergast—and we understand most of the officeholders in Kansas City and in the State government, besides members of the Senate and House of Representatives, are of your choosing—do you exact any promises in advance?"

"If a candidate hasn't got sense enough to see who helped him win and hasn't sense enough to recognize that man's friends, there is no use asking for favors from that candidate in advance."

"But a little bit more, Mr. Pendergast, about your methods, if you please."

"There are no alibis in politics. The delivery of the votes is what counts. And it is efficient organization in every little ward and precinct that determines national as well as local elections. . . . All the ballyhoo and showmanship such as they have at the national conventions is all right. It's a great show. It gives folks a run for their money. It makes everybody feel good. But the man who makes the organization possible is the man who delivers the votes, and he doesn't deliver them by oratory. Politics is a business, just like anything else."

"Thank you, Mr. Pendergast. We should like to ask a question or two more. We understand that Kansas City is one of the most wide-open towns in the United States. Is that true?"

"If by calling the city wide-open, you mean gambling and poker games where the poor man obtains his recreation just as the big men do in their clubs, it is wide-open. I wouldn't put a stop to it."

"A certain former lieutenant of yours, Mr. Pendergast, a man named Johnny Lazia, an ex-convict who was machine-gunned to death in July, 1934, was in trouble with the Federal income-tax authorities in 1933. The case was mysteriously hushed up for a while, but later, on demand of a Federal grand juror, it was prosecuted, and Lazia was convicted. Did you, on May 12, 1933, write this letter to Postmaster James A. Farley?

"Dear Jim:

Jerome Walsh and John Lazia will be in Washington to see you about the same matter that I had Mr. Kemper talk to you about. Now, Jim, Lazia is one of my chief lieutenants and I am more sincerely interested in his welfare than anything you might be able to do for me now or in the future. He has been in trouble with the Income Tax Department for some time. I know it was simply a case of being jobbed because of his Democratic activities. I think Frank Walsh spoke to the proper authorities about this. In any event, I wish you would use your utmost endeavor to bring about a settlement of this matter. I cannot make it any stronger, except to say that my interest in him is greater than anything that might come up in the future. Thanking you for any and everything you can do, I remain sincerely,

Your Friend,

T. J. Pendergast."

"Yes, I wrote it. I stand by it, too. I'd do it again and I'll stand by it."

Johnny Lazia's name keeps cropping up in this narrative. I think it is time we had a better look at him—closeup. Fred Allhoff, writing in *Liberty,* drew a pretty good picture of him.[1] "It is necessary—to understand the Kansas City of today—to go back to the tough First Ward. An Irishman named Michael Ross took up the reins there in the 1920's. Johnny Lazia, an Italian product of the North Side, deposed him and became boss. Lazia's chance came during a municipal bond election in 1928, when he and his henchmen abducted a number of Ross lieutenants. Lazia said later: 'Why not kidnap 'em? It doesn't hurt them and they can't hurt you.' Johnny Lazia in a few swift years became boss of the First Ward, close pal of Tom Pendergast, and a corpse. When, a few years ago, some ambushed machine gunners got him, every newspaper in Kansas City went maudlin. His obituaries were the most fantastic glorification of a gangster that has ever been set in sobbing type.

"For Lazia, when you brush away the adjectives, was little more than an ex-convict and gambler, a gum-chewing, weak-eyed egomaniac who had the First Ward and the whole Kansas City Police Department in his fingers . . . He became the 'fixer' of Kansas City, the man you went to if you wanted to run a racket in the heart of America. His yes or no was final . . . During the lush years his annual take on slot machines ran into seven figures . . . Grand Jury testimony has revealed that Johnny Lazia, ex-highway robber, actually made appointments to the Kansas City Police Department, and a G-man told of telephoning the office of the Director

[1] *Liberty*, Sept. 17, 1938. (One of a series of articles on Kansas City. Allhoff, along with numerous other writers, called upon me and my aides for information once it became clear that we were out to smash the Pendergast machine.)

of Police and finding his call answered, personally, by Johnny Lazia . . . 'I've done a lot for the Italians of Kansas City,' was one of his most frequent reminders."

Tom Pendergast did a lot for the Italians of Kansas City, too, chiefly by elevating such a character as Lazia to a position of power. This service to the Italians of the North Side did not go unrewarded. In October, 1938, Mussolini bestowed the Order of the Crown of Italy on Thomas Joseph Pendergast. Italian Vice-Consul Savorgnan, when placing the Order's medallion around the neck of the Kansas City boss, said: "Italians know their friends and how to show their gratitude." He went on to speak of the "silent but effective leader, whose deeds speak louder than words." Tom was really touched on this occasion, and no doubt sent his best regards to another dictator, Benito Mussolini.

When Pendergast was riding the crest of the political wave he derived a great deal of strength from an alliance forged with the Italian section of Kansas City, an area on the North Side known as "Little Italy." Most of the residents in this district were of Sicilian descent—85% in 1929. In a prejudiced Midwest community it was quite natural that "Little Italy" should acquire an evil name. It was said to be the hangout of underworld characters. Few non-residents dared to venture into its streets after dark. Wild tales were told of the crimes committed there. A great deal of this, of course, was the product of the imagination. In Kansas City anything foreign was under suspicion. That most of the families residing there were law-abiding, patriotic and harmless I have not the slightest doubt. I can agree with Giovanni Schiavo that, "If the

First Ward to some people is still a synonym for crime and degradation, the fault is not with the Italians. The First Ward, however, remains Kansas City's 'Little Italy' with all the fantastic publicity attached to it. In Kansas City, the Italian is made to suffer for the crimes of others. What a preposterous puritanism in a city that is so well acquainted with the activities of the Quantrill gangs and the James boys!!!" [1]

The majority of Kansas City's North Side Italians minded their own business, paid their bills, went to Mass, sent their children to school, and deported themselves in the manner of good citizens everywhere. Many of their houses were unpainted, were drab, and covered with soot, but inside was neatness, and cheer, traces of art and religion, and above all, music. But it was labeled "Underworld," and from the label grew the reality, for Prohibition and Pendergast brought a lot of undesirable characters to Kansas City who found sanctuary in "Little Italy." They enjoyed there the hospitality and the protection of Johnny Lazia. Dapper Lazia, soft-spoken and amiable, was a picture of innocence with his spats and cane and gloves (novelties that somewhat upset the political gatherings in rural Missouri when Lazia and other Pendergast delegates from Kansas City showed up) but he could be tough and cruel. He told the visiting gangsters from Chicago and St. Paul and other places that Pendergast wanted them to behave when they were in town—no messy crimes. In spite of this a lot of people were "taken for a ride" for one reason or another, and the victims of

[1] Giovanni Schiavo, *The Italians of Missouri,* New York, 1929.

gangland's feuds were found from time to time along Jackson County roads, where they had been unceremoniously dumped.

On the surface the link between Pendergast and Lazia was a natural one that caused no comment. The North Side Democratic Club was a regular party organization, and Lazia was its head. Giovanni Schiavo thought it was a success. He wrote: "It is since Mr. John Lazia organized the 'North Side Democratic Club' in 1928 that the Italians can really say that they have a political organization of which they can be proud. Prior to Mr. Lazia's advent the Italians cannot be said to have ever shown a united front. They were divided and did not count for much. They were simply satellites of the Irish political boss, Mr. 'Mike' Ross . . ."

For Pendergast—a medallion: Order of the Crown of Italy! In a short time, as we shall see, for Johnny Lazia—machine-gun bullets.

IV

BLOOD AND BALLOTS

Union Station Massacre

THE story of a dictator's decline and fall must begin, as a rule, far back in the record of his apparent glory. Even as the Order of the Crown of Italy was hung about Tom Pendergast's neck, that same neck was in jeopardy.

It seems to me that the story may best be told in three major episodes, for the details group themselves about these events in logic and time. The first of these grim and sordid adventures in American municipal politics entails the story of the Union Station Massacre.

On the evening of June 16, 1933, an Associated Press item carried the news that a man had been picked up in the White Front Pool Hall in Hot Springs, Arkansas, by three armed assailants. An air of mystery surrounded this incident. It was not known whether the disappearance of this unnamed man was an abduction or an arrest. His captors had sped with him towards Fort Smith.

At seven o'clock the next morning a Missouri Pacific train pulled into the Union Station in Kansas City. Three men, escorting a manacled prisoner got off. They were met by a number of grim-faced officers who seemed to be expecting them. They all walked silently through the station, stepped outside and headed for a parked automobile in the station plaza. They placed the prisoner in the car and were just getting in the car themselves when a voice a few feet away shouted, "Up, up!" This armed stranger, accompanied by two other men carrying machine guns, walked towards the car. At the first gesture of resistance the men carrying machine guns opened fire. The prisoner in the car slumped over the steering wheel, riddled with bullets. All but two of the group surrounding him lay dead or wounded. The crime known as the Union Station Massacre had taken place. There are men and women living today who would like to erase this bloody June 17, 1933, from their memory.

I shall try to reconstruct the crime. The prisoner whose bleeding body remained in the car was an escaped convict by the name of Frank "Jelly" Nash. The other dead were Chief of Police Otto Reed, of McAlester, Oklahoma, police officers W. J. Grooms and Frank Hermanson of Kansas City, and Special Agent Raymond J. Caffrey of the Federal Bureau of Investigation. Special Agents F. J. Lackey and Frank Smith miraculously escaped unharmed.

Nash had escaped from the Federal Penitentiary at Leavenworth, Kansas, on October 19, 1930. Since that date he had engaged in a number of bank robberies and other crimes. Previously he had served prison terms in Oklahoma for murder, burglarly, assault and other evil deeds, but he was pardoned and set free in each instance. His escape from Leavenworth came about as the result of a carefully laid plan. He had been made a trusty in reward for good behavior and was allowed to go outside the prison walls on occasion. He tried to make himself a model prisoner so that he could win more special privileges. One day he got an outside assignment, and simply walked away. Call it prison laxity, misplaced trust, or what you will—the fact remained that a desperate criminal was at large, and a nation-wide man hunt was on.

"Jelly" Nash, we learned later, had gone to Joplin, Missouri, after his escape, and spent a few days with Herbert Farmer. Farmer had been in the Oklahoma State Penitentiary with Nash, and their meeting in Joplin was a reunion. Later, Nash went to Chicago, where he was often seen in the O.P. Inn, operated by his friend "Doc" Stacey. In Stacey's tavern he met a comely brunette named Frances Luce, who worked there, and he fell in love with her and married her. The fact that he had an undivorced wife living elsewhere made little or no difference. Nash had covered his bald head with a toupee, and bore little resemblance to the portrait on the "Reward Offered" posters. He and his new bride went to Hot Springs, Arkansas, to play the races and to relax in the friendly atmosphere of that city. He was a frequent visitor to the White Front Pool Hall, run by Richard Tallman Galatas, who was strongly entrenched with the local police department. Like Johnny Lazia in Kansas City, Galatas could guarantee protection to underworld characters as long as they remained reasonably quiet and curbed their homicidal tendencies. He took a liking to "Jelly" Nash, but warned him now and then to refrain from a public display of his talents. Nash loved a good time, and with a few drinks under his belt, became the life of the party. He sang rather well, and on occasion he would grab the baton from the "hot spot" band leader and do a bit of clowning.

The FBI got a tip that Nash was in Hot Springs, and they traced him to the White Front Pool Hall. They recognized him and pounced on him in a rather unceremonious manner, roughing him up a bit in the process. They knew that he had police protection so they bundled him into a car and raced out of town. This was the incident that gave rise to the Associated Press item referred to at the head of this chapter.

The two FBI men, Lackey and Smith, accompanied by Chief of Police Reed, of McAlester, Oklahoma, planned originally to drive the captured Nash all the way to Kansas City, but a series of mysterious events changed their minds. Entering Benton, Arkansas, their car was stopped by police officers. They explained that they had been advised by telephone that a man had been kidnapped at Hot Springs. Lackey and Smith flashed their identification cards and were allowed to proceed on their way. The same thing happened in exactly the same manner when they reached Little Rock, except that on this occasion the local officers gave them a police escort to the city limits. At Fort Smith, the captors of Nash stopped and held a conference. They put through a call to Kansas City and were advised to transfer their "hot" prisoner to the Missouri Pacific train at Fort Smith and to proceed in that manner to Kansas City, where reinforcements were promised.

The arrival in Kansas City was as scheduled. Special Agent Vetterli of the Kansas City office of the FBI was on the station platform to meet the train, as were police officers Grooms and Hermanson. The six men walked through the station and out into the station plaza as heretofore described. As they were being ambushed by the three gangsters, one of the party, officer Grooms, fired at and wounded one of the thugs. He had no sooner fired than the leader of the desperadoes shouted, "Let 'em have it!" The handcuffed Nash cried out, "Don't shoot me!" but he was one of the first to die. "They're all dead here," observed the leader, and his two companions watched him edge up to the car and peer inside. They ceased firing, and before anyone could positively identify them they jumped in a car and fled. The crowd in the station plaza was stunned. During the battle many had run for cover. Others stood transfixed in their tracks, too scared to move a muscle.

The Union Station Massacre was headlined throughout the nation that day and for many days thereafter. An interested reader of the news was "Boss" Tom Pendergast. He could steal an election with no qualms of conscience, but he could not condone the murder of unarmed agents of the Government in a public place in broad daylight. People would point to this crime and say, "What can you expect in a town where a boss-controlled police department plays ball with underworld characters like Johnny Lazia?" This was just the kind of messy crime that Lazia promised Pendergast he would keep out of Kansas City. It gave the "machine" a black eye and it hurt Kansas City beyond measure. Pendergast's worst fears were soon realized. People did talk, and newspaper editors asked a lot of questions that no one in high places could satisfactorily answer. City Manager McElroy and Chief of Police Reppert came out with a statement to the effect that they had reliable information proving that the Union Station

Massacre was not perpetrated by local gangsters, and that since it was obviously an "outside" job Kansas City's responsibility for the crime was considerably lessened. This flimsy reasoning did not satisfy the Federal Government. One of its trusted agents had been killed, another wounded. The FBI was determined to track the killers down if it took years.

Days went by without any tangible clues as to the identity of the three killers. The motive back of the crime was not established. If these desperate men were trying to "spring" Nash, why did they shoot him? Were they afraid he might "squeal" on them? How did they know that the men sent to meet the Missouri Pacific train on that fatal morning were inadequately armed? This latter point gave the FBI men something to think about. Why had officers Hermanson and Grooms been allowed to go on duty that morning without the machine guns they invariably carried in their car? It was revealed that Federal agents had requested help from the Kansas City Police Department in bringing the convict Nash safely through the city on his way to Leavenworth. They explained that he was a desperate criminal. Grooms and Hermanson were normally assigned to patrol duty in the business district and were warned to be on the lookout for bank robbers. They had a special car equipped with machine guns. They never went on tour of duty without these guns. Yet, for some mysterious reason, on the morning of the Union Station Massacre, Grooms and Hermanson were sent out with no machine guns in their car. Asked later to explain how this happened, the police department officials simply shrugged their shoulders, and threw up their hands and as much as said, "It's just one of those things."

The case remained unsolved. A year passed. Still no clues that put the finger on the actual killers. By that time I had been appointed U.S. District Attorney. As soon as I took office I asked the Government men to brief me on the progress of the investigation into the Union Station Massacre. We studied all the clues again. I threw the full weight of my office behind the investigation. Frankly, we were stymied, and we were discouraged every time a new clue took us down a blind alley. Witnesses gave completely conflicting descriptions of what took place on that June morning in 1933.

But we did not give up. The hard-working and resourceful FBI men accepted this unsolved crime as a challenge. My admiration for their skill and tenacity increased daily. This baffling case occupied more and more of my time. As long as the three killers were at large my office was on the spot, and I knew it. The FBI agents decided to retrace their steps from the very beginning of their investigation. They questioned everything anew. Why had the captors of Nash been questioned by the police as they sped through Arkansas? Who sent those mysterious telephone calls informing the police that a man had been kidnapped in Hot Springs? Some sinister force had been at work that day. How sinister it was became all too apparent when machine guns blazed in the beautiful station plaza in Kansas City the following morning. The FBI went to Hot Springs and checked with the telephone company. It developed that long distance calls had been made on June 16, 1933, from Hot Springs to Little Rock, Joplin and Chicago. Richard T. Galatas, owner of the

White Front Pool Hall, had made the calls to the police in Benton and Little Rock. This same Galatas, in the company of Mrs. Frank Nash, had made long distance calls to Joplin and Chicago. The next step was to ascertain who answered those calls, and what conversation took place.

It was learned that Galatas had gone into action as soon as Nash had been picked up. He first notified Mrs. Nash that her husband had been spirited away. He then made contact with "Dutch" Akers, Chief of Detectives of Hot Springs, and asked Akers to come to his house for a conference. Akers and Galatas had been working a number of rackets, and as a token of appreciation for his "take" in these nefarious practices Akers gave Galatas and his friends "protection." It was proved that Galatas and Mrs. Nash put through calls to the O.P. Inn in Chicago and to Herbert and Esther Farmer in Joplin.

The FBI on that harried auto trip through Arkansas had let it be known that they were driving to Joplin. That they changed their minds and boarded a train the reader knows by this time. Galatas hired a plane in Hot Springs, and he and Mrs. Nash were flown to Joplin, where they were to be met by Farmer and his wife. From Farmer's house a call went out to Vernon C. Miller, in Kansas City. It was further determined that a call had been made from a pay station in the Union Station in Kansas City to the home of Herbert Farmer in Joplin. It was also discovered that a call had been made from the O.P. Inn in Chicago to the residence of one "Fritz" Mulloy in Kansas City, and that a return call was made from Vernon C. Miller's address to "Doc" Stacey's O.P.

Inn in Chicago. Gangland had kept the wires hot on the night preceding the Union Station Massacre.

It was now obvious to all of us connected with the investigation that "Jelly" Nash's friends had actually tried to "spring" him from the clutches of the law, and that this abortive attempt had ended in wholesale murder.

The question now before the FBI was the exact whereabouts of all the persons involved in those telephone calls. Hot Springs was combed, but Galatas and his wife had disappeared over night. The Farmers were not to be located in Joplin, and no one could furnish a clue as to their whereabouts. The widow of Frank Nash was likewise in hiding. Vernon C. "Verne" Miller and his paramour, Vivian Mathias, had suddenly left their Kansas City bungalow where they had been living for several months under assumed names. Right after the Union Station Massacre the household goods of Miller had been taken in a truck and delivered to the home of "Fritz" Mulloy. When the agents searched the Miller premises they found a vacant house. In the rubbish in the basement were a few empty beer bottles. Slim pickings, but on second thought one of the agents picked up a beer bottle. On it was found a tell-tale mark which was to later identify one of the killers.

The day before the massacre an interesting incident took place which added to the mystery. On the morning of June 16th, Sheriff Jack Killingsworth of Bolivar, Missouri, went to a public garage and accidentally encountered Charles "Pretty Boy" Floyd and Adam Richetti, notorious bank robbers and killers from the Cookson Hills of Oklahoma. These desperadoes were wanted in several states.

Covering Killingsworth with their guns they forced him into a car and made him drive them on to the highway. After going a few miles the bandits told the captured sheriff to pull up by the side of the road and stop. All three got out and Floyd and Richetti held up a traveling salesman who happened to drive by. They commandeered the salesman's car and drove with the sheriff and the salesman in the direction of Kansas City, arriving there at night, where they released their captives. They then took cover in some unknown hideout. This was the night before the tragedy. The FBI were puzzled. They could produce no evidence which would link Floyd and Richetti with Nash. Their activities had been entirely separate. Their trails had not even crossed. Moreover, there was not one bit of evidence to show that Floyd and Richetti had participated in the Union Station Massacre.

Only one person saw any possible link between the two circumstances—the coincidental presence of Floyd and Richetti in Kansas City the night before the crime took place. She was Mrs. Lottie West, the woman in charge of the Travelers Aid desk at the entrance of the Union Station. She was experienced in meeting the public and she prided herself on being able to remember names and faces. She liked to study the faces in the ever-shifting crowd in the busy station lobby. On the morning of the massacre she was impressed by the cruel face of a man who sat motionless and silent a few feet away. He seemed to be waiting for some grim eventuality. Being a friendly and helpful person by nature and training Mrs. West sought to engage the morose stranger in conversation, but he maintained a dogged silence and kept his eyes riveted on the gates where the de-training passengers came out to the platform abutting the streets. Mrs. West finally gave up trying to get the stranger to talk, but his face and manner remained fixed in her memory. She went about her business and for the moment dismissed the young man from her mind. The next time she saw him was when the three killers were surrounding the car of Special Agent Caffrey and pointing their machine guns at the officers. Mrs. West witnessed the slaying. She sought a policeman, and pointing to the scene of the shooting she identified one of the fleeing killers as the young man she had seen earlier that morning, and shouted to officer Fanning, "Shoot him before he gets away!" Officer Fanning drew his pistol and fired, but the shot went wide of its mark. We showed Mrs. West a number of photographs. "That's the one!" she said excitedly. It was a photograph of Charles "Pretty Boy" Floyd. Although she recalled that she had seen three men doing the killing, she was unable to identify two of them, for her attention was riveted upon the mysterious stranger she had tried so unsuccessfully to talk to that fatal morning. This, we agreed, was quite natural under the circumstances. Some of the FBI men were skeptical about Mrs. West's identification. To connect "Pretty Boy" Floyd with this murder just didn't make sense. Other "positive" identifications had turned out to be false, and probably Mrs. West's story was no better than the others.

Within a month following the crime, Herbert Farmer and his wife had been located and arrested. Mrs. Frank Nash was later taken into custody in Illinois. "Fritz" Mulloy and "Doc" Stacey were also apprehended. The whereabouts of Verne Miller, Richard Galatas and wife, remained undisclosed. The nationwide search for them continued.

Under "positive" identification of witnesses, Harvey Bailey, Robert Brady and Wilbur Underhill were included in the indictment first returned in this celebrated case, but no mention was made of either "Pretty Boy" Floyd or Adam Richetti. Further investigation showed that Bailey, Brady and Underhill could not have been involved in the murder. The FBI placed less and less faith in Mrs. West's story about "Pretty Boy" Floyd after these similar ironclad identifications proved to be duds. The one man who might produce the missing links in the case was "Dick" Galatas, and he could not be found. The agents began a detailed study of his past.

Galatas had begun his career in Chicago, working as a bank clerk. He held other honest jobs, but finally drifted into bad company and became interested in the confidence game racket which he worked under various names in Chicago, Milwaukee, Detroit and other places. He then went to California where he started riding coastwise passenger ships, playing cards and continuing his old operations. He then started riding trains. He went to Montreal, where he took ship for Cuba. He made several ocean trips, but became afflicted with rheumatism. Someone suggested that he try the baths at Hot Springs, Arkansas. For a number of years he was in and out of Hot Springs, and he struck up a friendship with "Dutch" Akers, whom I have mentioned previously. In his usual persuasive and debonair manner Galatas made himself "solid" with the Hot Springs police and carried on his gambling without molestation. His White Front Pool

Hall became the rendezvous of the "con" men and "big shot" gamblers, and handbooks on the races were carried on there with the approval of "Dutch" Akers. By 1933 his influence was at its zenith.

When Frank "Jelly" Nash blew into Hot Springs he struck up a profitable friendship with Galatas. His rich baritone voice was often heard in the White Front Pool Hall. Verne Miller, the bandit, met Galatas through Nash. This made an interesting trio: the smooth Galatas, the gay Nash, and the quiet Miller, who looked anything but the killer and bank robber that he was, with his slight stature, his steel gray eyes, and his gentle manner with women.

Verne Miller had had an unusual career. He returned from the First World War a decorated hero. The people in his home town in South Dakota were very proud of him, and elected him to office. Before his term had ended he was charged with embezzlement of public funds and was tried and convicted. After serving a term in prison he began a reckless career of running illicit liquor over the border from Canada. He did a flourishing business, but ran afoul of the law and was once more brought before the bar of justice. He "hopped" his bond and became a fugitive. He joined the "Purple Gang" in Detroit. This gang terrorized Detroit and vicinity, and had powerful contacts with the New York underworld. In 1933 the spotlight of law enforcement was turned upon the "Purple Gang" and its members were forced to go into hiding to escape the "heat."

Meanwhile Miller had attached himself to a pretty blonde whose alias at that particular time was Vivian Mathias. He took her with him when he skipped from

Detroit, and after a short stay in Chicago the couple moved to Kansas City, the town where Johnny Lazia offered hospitable welcome to "strangers" who wanted to go into "business" on his terms. "Don't abuse my hospitality," he said to trigger-nervous guests. At that time Kansas City, center station of the Crime Corridor, harbored as odd an assortment of talented transients as you would ever wish to avoid. Pendergast and his "boys" were riding the crest of prosperity. A messy crime like the Union Station Massacre was bad for "business." It meant that G-Men would swoop down on the town like a pack of bloodhounds.

At any event Verne Miller and his paramour enjoyed a brief interlude of happiness in their Kansas City bungalow. For protection they took the name of Moore. Mr. Moore, who loved the ancient and honorable game of golf, joined one of the more fashionable golf clubs. It has been said that some of Miller's guests carried guns in their golf bags—just in case. "Doc" Stacey, owner of the O.P. Inn in Chicago, ran down to Kansas City occasionally for a round or two of golf with Miller. It was on one of these visits that Miller introduced Stacey to Johnny Lazia, "whom I understood to be a big shot politician," Stacey later confessed.

Unless you knew Verne Miller you might judge him to be slightly effeminate. Women liked him. He was most decorous in his treatment of them. He would permit no vulgarity in their presence. When he turned his gray eyes upon men using profane language and said, "Cut it!" they immediately changed the subject. Considering the character of some of Miller's associates this gallantry of his must have imposed considerable restraint upon their speech habits. But he was no man to argue with.

To continue with my cast of characters a word or two about "Pretty Boy" Floyd may not be amiss at this point. His criminal record dated back to September 16, 1925, when he was sentenced to serve five years in the Missouri State Penitentiary for highway robbery. He completed this sentence, and shortly thereafter was arrested in Kansas City, Kansas, as well as in Kansas City, Missouri, but after being investigated was released by the Kansas and Missouri officials. His criminal career took him to Pueblo, Colorado, where he was sentenced to jail. Later he was sentenced for a bank robbery in Toledo, Ohio, but en route to the Ohio State Penitentiary, where he was scheduled to spend the next ten or fifteen years of his life, he escaped and became a fugitive from justice, like Verne Miller.

"Pretty Boy" Floyd eventually met up with a kindred soul by the name of Adam Richetti. Richetti's criminal record dates back to 1928. He was involved in a holdup at Crown Point, Indiana. After doing time he was charged with bank robbery in Oklahoma, jumped his bond and became a hunted man. After he and Floyd became partners in crime they betook themselves to the Cookson Hills, in Oklahoma. Fabulous legends have arisen from their frequent visits to that hideout. To many settlers in that wild area "Pretty Boy" Floyd was pictured as a kind of Robin Hood, preying on the rich and bestowing alms upon the poor. The brutality of Floyd removed much of this glamour. He murdered two brothers by the names of William and Wallace Ash in Kansas City, Kansas, in 1931

—the motive being that he was madly in love with the wife of one of the brothers. He shot Ralph Castner, a police officer at Bowling Green, Ohio, while resisting arrest for robbing a bank in Mount Zion, Kentucky. The finger of guilt pointed to the brutal murder of Curtis C. Burks, a Federal Prohibition Agent, in Kansas City, Missouri, during a raid. A spectator was also killed by Floyd during this same episode. Witnesses say that Floyd killed Irvin Kelley, a deputy sheriff, when that officer tried to arrest him near Pacific, Oklahoma. The record is long and gruesome. The FBI, following the Union Station Massacre in Kansas City, went into the Cookson Hills in Oklahoma, hoping to find traces of Floyd and Richetti. They simply were not to be found, and some of the natives wouldn't talk.

During all this time the search for the other missing characters continued. The FBI learned that Verne Miller and Vivian Mathias were in Chicago, and a trap was set for their capture, but Miller escaped in a running gun battle. Vivian Mathias was arrested in the apartment she and Miller had been occupying, and charges were filed against her for harboring a fugitive from justice. She was sentenced to prison for a year and a day. Her arrest and conviction developed no new leads as to the murderers involved in the Union Station Massacre. She refused to talk and took her punishment with grim stoicism. Miller had escaped, and the trail had cooled.

Weeks passed. One morning on a lonely road just outside of Detroit a nude body was found, bundled in a blanket and lying at the opening of a drain under a railroad embankment. The blanket revealed no marks of identification whatsoever, but the fingerprints of the mangled body proved that the career of Vernon C. Miller had come to its bloody close. Like many a man who had entered a life of crime he met death at the hands of his own gang. All friendship ceases when some criminal with the "heat" on him brings the pursuing pack too close for comfort, or when he "knows too much." Under the code of the underworld this sudden liquidation was the last resort in solving a difficult problem. From the facts and circumstances of Miller's death the FBI concluded that the "Purple Gang" in Detroit had found Miller's return to their midst a trifle embarrassing.

Miller's death left us with an unsolved mystery. What he might have revealed about the Union Station Massacre would never be spoken. One avenue of approach was definitely ended. Men like Miller do not leave diaries and scrapbooks. The search for Floyd and Richetti and for Galatas and wife was intensified.

In a weekly magazine printed in the East appeared each week a column of criminals wanted. In one issue were pictures of alleged fugitives from justice. A reward was offered for their apprehension. A man in New Orleans read that page and fixed the pictures in his mind. He never expected to meet up with any of them. One day while entering a building he noticed a handsome man with hair graying at the temples and with soft gray eyes. The face seemed familiar. He followed him into an elevator and down a corridor. Suddenly he remembered the faces he had seen in the magazine. He was sure of the man's identity now. It was Galatas. He quickly reported the incident to the FBI, and Galatas and his wife were arrested. The jaws of the trap were closing in.

Meanwhile, the FBI made an important discovery in Kansas City. The fingerprints on the empty beer bottle picked up in Verne Miller's bungalow turned out to be those of Adam Richetti. This seemed to link Richetti with Miller. It now seemed reasonable to suppose that Richetti had visited Miller prior to the Union Station Massacre, and if Richetti was there it was highly probable that "Pretty Boy" Floyd was there, too, for they had become almost inseparable companions. We were in a high state of excitement.

Mrs. Nash broke her long silence and began to talk. She told how Dick Galatas had come to her that day in Hot Springs to inform her that her husband had been picked up by the law and hustled out of town. She told how she and Galatas had put through a call to "Doc" Stacey in Chicago advising him of the capture; how Galatas had been tipped off by "Dutch" Akers that the officers were headed for Joplin with Nash in custody. The plane trip to Joplin was an attempt to intercept the officers and "spring" Nash, but they learned that the officers had changed their mind and got on a train at Fort Smith. At the home of Herbert and Esther Farmer in Joplin, Frances Nash talked on the telephone with Verne Miller in Kansas City. She was weeping, and Miller tried to comfort her. He told her not to worry, that he would take care of the situation in Kansas City. At midnight Miller called her from the Union Station in Kansas City to reassure her, saying that plans had already been made. The next morning Frances Nash heard about the Union Station Massacre over the radio. Miller called her again, but Esther Farmer took the message. Miller left instructions that Frances Nash was to go to his Chicago apartment and remain there until she heard from him. Frances Nash refused to take this order and went to the home of relatives in Winona, Illinois instead, broken by the tragedy and fearful of being arrested. For a long time "Jelly" had not told her about the occupation of some of the friends he introduced her to, and she was not aware of the full extent of her husband's lawlessness. All she remembered was the round of night club parties, trips to New York, visits to resorts and race tracks. Sometimes "Jelly" made trips alone. When he returned from them with "fresh" money, a term used by criminals engaged in perilous undertakings, she knew that this meant a gay spending spree in Hot Springs. When she did find out about her husband's career of crime she remained loyal to him.

This confession by Frances Nash proved to the FBI that Verne Miller was one of the killers they had long been seeking. Who the other two were remained a mystery. When Galatas was questioned he substantiated the facts given by Frances Nash. Neither Galatas nor Mrs. Nash could name the two killers still unaccounted for, and if they knew they kept the secret to themselves.

An interesting sidelight occurred, having no direct bearing on the case in question—at least not on the surface, but out of which were to come disclosures which were destined to supply the missing link in a chain of circumstances that finally brought a solution to the mystery. At midnight on a warm August night in 1934, three men stepped from an ambush in front of a fashionable apartment house in Kansas City and riddled the body of Johnny Lazia with machine gun bullets. The friend of Pendergast and boss of the Kansas City underworld had met his end. Pendergast and McElroy sent floral wreaths. Over two hundred cars formed the funeral procession.

Shortly after Lazia's death an attempt was made upon the life of James LaCapra. He had been a friend of Johnny Lazia, but we later discovered that some of Lazia's followers thought that LaCapra "knew too much" about their leader. The first attempt upon the life of LaCapra failed, for he ran into the Post Office just in the nick of time. The men who were out to get him made a second attempt, but once more they were unsuccessful. Thoroughly frightened by these sinister attempts to remove him from the scene, LaCapra gave himself up as a violator of the Dyer Act and was taken into custody by the Federal Government.

During his stay in jail LaCapra revealed to the investigators that on the evening of June 16, 1933, Verne Miller had approached John Lazia and advised him that a friend of his was in the custody of officers and that he desired to have him "sprung" in Kansas City the following morning. Miller asked Lazia to furnish him with men from the Kansas City underworld to assist him in this job. Lazia told Miller that he did not wish to furnish any of his own men for such a job. The risk was too great. He did tell Miller, however, that Charles "Pretty Boy" Floyd and Adam Richetti had just blown into town, that they were being harbored by friends of his, and that he could arrange a meeting that night between Floyd, Richetti and Miller. He added, "They would be the very men for the job." LaCapra further revealed that Lazia brought Miller in contact with the two fugitives that very night as he had promised, and that the next morning Miller, Floyd and Richetti drove in one car to the Union Station to await the arrival of the Special Agents who were returning Frank Nash to prison. The plan was to intimidate the officers with a display of machine guns, forcing them to set Nash free. When Officer Grooms resisted and fired at "Pretty Boy" Floyd, wounding him in the shoulder, Miller and Richetti opened fire, and the wounded Floyd also began firing at the officers. In this sudden hail of bullets Nash was accidentally killed. The plan to gain his release had gone haywire. The bravado of officer Grooms in the face of almost certain death messed up their strategy. They must have been tipped off by Lazia that Grooms and Hermanson were not equipped with their usual machine guns, and they knew that the FBI men were not armed, as was the custom prior to that fatal shooting. This was the crime which convinced the Federal Bureau of Investigation that its operatives should be fully prepared to resist attack.

What happened to James LaCapra who recited these facts to the Government? He fled to New York to escape the vengeance of Lazia's followers. He was later found along a New York highway with a bullet hole through his forehead. Gang reprisal had caught up with him.

Following rapidly upon these disclosures, police officers in a small town in Ohio on a routine tour of inspection of a city park saw a couple of sleeping figures lying on the ground. They awakened them and began questioning them, since they appeared to be strangers. One of these men drew a gun and began firing at the officers. The other took to his heels and escaped. The man who did the shooting was subdued and put in jail, where he made every effort to disguise his identity. His captors took his finger prints and had them checked. He turned out to be Adam Richetti. By inference, considering former crimes, his fleeing companion must have been "Pretty Boy" Floyd. The FBI swung into action and rushed to the spot near East Liverpool where the trail seemed hot. The Federal Agents, led by Melvin H. Purvis, the nemesis of so many gangsters, cornered Floyd in a lonely farm house some seven miles from East Liverpool. Floyd tried to flee, but fifty or more shots rang out and he fell mortally wounded, unable to use the two automatic pistols he was carrying. The officers rushed up to his prostrate body. "Who the hell tipped you?" he gasped. He struggled to gain enough breath to speak. "Where is Eddie?" he inquired. Those were his last words.

My office asked for the return of Adam Richetti to Kansas City to stand trial for participation in the Union Station Massacre. At no time did he admit his guilt. We had information showing that the night following the crime Floyd and Richetti were supplied with transportation and an escort out of town.

After leaving Kansas City in the car supplied by friends of Johnny Lazia, Floyd and Richetti drove to Cleveland, and from there they went to Buffalo, New York, where they shared an apartment with two women for several months. Ennui drove them from their hideout and they set out for their beloved Cookson Hills, in Oklahoma. They were accidentally apprehended in Ohio in the manner previously described. Richetti was brought to trial, convicted, and duly executed, paying his debt to society for his part in the Union Station Massacre.

The case did not end there. The conspirators were also brought to trial. At the beginning of the trial Vivian Mathias entered a plea of guilty. Frances Nash took the stand and detailed to the jury her part in the plot. For this aid to the Government in the prosecution of the case she was granted immunity. Galatas denied any connection with the affair, maintaining the suave attitude of the "con" man to the end. Herbert and Esther Farmer, "Doc" Stacey, "Fritz" Mulloy, and Elizabeth Galatas were the other defendants. The jury returned a verdict of guilty against all of them. Galatas, Farmer and Mulloy were sentenced to Alcatraz, Stacey (Louis Stacci) was sentenced to Leavenworth. Due to her plea of guilty and having served a term for harboring Verne Miller the court extended probation to Vivian Mathias as well as to Elizabeth Galatas and Esther Farmer.

Thus came to a close the chain of events heralded by the brief Associated Press story of June 16, 1933, which announced the kidnapping or capture of a man in the White Front Pool Hall in Hot Springs. Eight men were killed—four officers of the law, four fugitives from justice. Four men were placed behind prison bars. The deaths of LaCapra and Lazia, and several others whose names have not even been mentioned in this chapter, may have resulted from connection with the series of episodes growing out of the Union Station Massacre. Its repercussions were felt throughout the entire underworld of the United States.

VOTE FRAUDS

FATE moved another step closer to the Boss. The death of Johnny Lazia was the first indication of a loosening grip. The second was the success of the Federal authorities in the investigation and punishment of wholesale vote frauds in Jackson County, Missouri.

Tom Pendergast, like City Manager McElroy, had his own system of arithmetic. He could produce two votes where only one was legal. This talent enabled him to rule Kansas City without serious opposition for years. Pendergast, as head of the Jackson County Democratic Club, could name his own local slate and elect each candidate by a landslide vote. Through connections in Jefferson City and the various county seats he could name State officials, as well as delegates to the Democratic National Conventions. It was a foregone conclusion that Pendergast would not be satisfied until he had his own Senator in Washington.

It might interest the reader to know the mechanics of Pendergast's political juggernaut and the expert technique used in its operation. His organization was fashioned like Tammany Hall and in its infancy took many a lesson from the "Old Hall" which so long dominated the political affairs of New York City. In its maturity the Kansas City machine could have taught the Tammany Tiger many new tricks.

Pendergast was a realist. He left nothing to chance. His political judgment was almost uncanny; his decisions were reached swiftly with exactness. The adherents of his cause followed him with almost fanatical fervor and few were courageous enough to question the wisdom of his acts or to weigh the ultimate consequences. No army was ever better recruited, disciplined and trained than was his political organization. Every district was captained by experienced strategists, and on election day his troops were marshaled by hundreds of skilled workers in the wards and precincts of the polling places. As Napoleon's legions traveled upon their bellies so was Pendergast's army fed upon patronage, jobs being the life blood of any political army.

By the election machinery of the city, political units were divided into districts or wards or precincts. Most ward leaders held some important city or county office; and the retention of his position depended upon a man's ability to deliver a majority of the votes in his ward on election day. This was an open invitation to fraudulent practices, and Pendergast did not ask them to explain their methods just so long as the expected quota of votes was produced. In this respect he allowed them to exercise a great deal of initiative. The wards of the city were divided into precincts and the contact man in each precinct was a sub-boss known as the precinct captain.

Precinct captains were for the most part on the city or county payroll. The work of each precinct captain was a three hundred and sixty-five days a year job. It was his duty to cultivate the good will of the voters in his territory, to look after the interests of those who showed a willingness to follow the flag of the boss on election day. Each captain had a fund provided him by the "organization" upon which he could draw to aid the needy in time of want or suffering. Tom learned this trick from his brother Jim back in the old days. He would line up a bunch of derelicts in front of the polling place at an early hour and keep them contented by passing around cups of steaming coffee. Each year at Christmas, Councilman Charlie Clark, an old-line politician, arranged a big dinner on the North Side for down-and-outers, remarking as he passed around the turkey, "We are guests of Tom Pendergast." The precinct captain was also a personal relations man who met each new resident and saw to it that the water was turned on and the gas and electric hook-ups made promptly by the utility companies. It was in the line of duty to make sure that each new resident was duly registered on the rolls of the election books. These industrious captains were not good Samaritans in the sense commonly associated with that term: they were clever politicians trading favors for votes. The solicitude of the precinct captains was not confined to newcomers. It was their job to keep in touch with the old established families, and if any of these "friends" and "neighbors" ran afoul of the law it was their duty to see that bond was arranged and that no harsh treatment was meted out by city and county officials. If a son or daughter got a ticket for some traffic violation the helpful precinct worker was ready to speak to the proper person.

Any applicant for political office had to have the endorsement of the precinct captain before his candidacy could be considered. On election day cars were provided for the transportation of the voters to the polls and scores of precinct workers met the voters and handed them sample ballots conveniently marked so that there would be no misunderstanding as to the names of the "best" candidates. Pendergast's philosophy was "get out the votes in the precincts and the wards will take care of themselves."

Hundreds of city employees were enlisted in the ranks of Pendergast's army on election day. The underworld contributed money and manpower to promote the success of the machine. Houses of vice sent its inmates forth on election day to do the bidding of the organization. Gamblers, protected racketeers and vice lords "kicked in" to put the Pendergast candidates in office. Even the members of the police department were forced to contribute a part of their annual salaries to the "cause." Pendergast himself, ever eager to win support, passed out dollars and half dollars to lines of indigent callers who formed at his office on Main Street. His "generosity" became legendary.

Getting out the vote is a normal function of all political organizations. Helping voters to get to the polls and doing favors for them comes under the head of commonsense. Had the Pendergast machine confined itself to these perfectly legitimate activities no one could have raised a serious protest. Had the votes been honestly counted no one would have objected to the Pendergast manner of winning friends and influencing people. Bear in mind that many of the votes were honest. But in a close election these honest votes were not sufficient to offset the strength of the opposition. Corrupt election officials, working hand in hand with Pendergast's lieutenants, ran in "ghost" votes, that is to say names of deceased persons, fictitious names, names taken from false registration lists. If it became necessary to nullify some of the honest votes by erasing names and substituting others this could be conveniently arranged behind the scenes. Since each precinct had a certain quota of votes to deliver for each of the Pendergast candidates it was hardly necessary to go to all the trouble of counting the votes. These are serious charges. I do not toss them around lightly. As this chapter unfolds I shall cite specific instances.

Not only were the Kansas City elections fraudulent, they were accompanied by intimidation, coercion and violence.

Less than two months after I became U.S. District Attorney I witnessed the municipal election of 1934, called the "Bloody Election." It was an illuminating experience. I discovered that the methods of Fascism were not confined to Germany and Italy. It was after this election that Jesse W. Barrett, Republican candidate for Governor of Missouri, told a Kansas City audience: "We all remember the pictures of the hospital wards filled with men who were broken and bruised by the gangsters who assaulted them at the polls. You remember that flood of fraudulent votes. You were baptised in blood, but the contest was won by the machine. The score was four murders, two hundred assaults, and one hundred thousand felonies."

Intermittent sniping at machine-controlled city government (a boss-ridden setup under the direction of City Manager McElroy) had been going on for some time, but just before the 1934 municipal election this indignant opposition culminated in an organized Fusionist group made up of Republicans and non-machine Democrats. The spearhead of the movement was the National Youth Movement. The Fusionists were a militant, well-informed, progressive and decent group. The Fusion ticket was headed by men of impeccable character, including Dr. A. Ross Hill, former President of the University of Missouri, who was chosen as the candidate for Mayor. Some of the younger members of the group were vigorous in their denunciation of the Pendergast machine. They painted a true picture of the graft, corruption and inefficiency of the Pendergast-McElroy type of city government. The local press supported the reform movement. It looked like a determined effort to crush Pendergastism at the polls. Poll watchers would be on hand to prevent irregularities, and the Kansas City *Star* was sending out a field force of reporters and cameramen to get documentary evidence of attempted fraud.

Pendergast was not frightened by all this, but he was shrewdly on the alert. He sent word down the line that this election "has to be won or else." Tension mounted. When the polls opened at 6 a.m., March 27, 1934, the whole town sensed that excitement was in the air and that the contest at the polls would be a bitter one. No one knew how bloody and shameful it was to be—no one but the machine-instructed hoodlums who were given orders to "do a job" on the Fusionist adherents.

The pattern for the day's activities became apparent before the polls had been opened two hours. It was obvious that Pendergast was determined to win the election at all costs. No sporting gestures came from his headquarters on that memorable day. His cohorts had a well-integrated political powerhouse at their disposal; every precinct was organized to the nth degree; over 50,000 "ghost" names were on the padded registration lists, but still the boss was fearful that decency might prevail in spite of his precautions. He was taking no chances.

Cars without license plates began to show up on the streets. They were filled with "hoods," the local term for hoodlums. They were an ugly-looking bunch of men. Most of them carried firearms. The Fusion headquarters was in the heart of the Kansas City business district. It was alive with early morning activity. Party workers talked hopefully of a stunning political upset. The proverbial big black car without tags drove by the Fusion headquarters and seven bullets were fired through the plate glass window of the office. Those in the office miraculously escaped injury. But they knew that gangland had posted notice of its intention to intimidate the electorate.

Shortly thereafter the cruising band of thugs rushed into the Ninth Ward headquarters of the Fusionists and assaulted with gun butts and blackjacks three persons who were harming no one. One of the cars in the gangland motorcade was equipped with a siren. The slugging was in retaliation for the persistency of one Fusion worker who asked for and received a third poll book after two others had been taken from her and destroyed.

Justin D. Bowersock, a reporter for the *Star,* was assigned to investigate election irregularities. He observed three cars loaded with "repeaters" being driven from one polling place to another. A car filled with thugs forced his own car to the curb. Some of the thugs got out, walked over to Bowersock's car and yanked him out by grabbing him by the necktie. Then they beat him with the butts of their guns. Two men who happened to be in Bowersock's car at the time were also slugged. Bowersock jumped on the running board of a passing car and screamed to the driver to rush him to the *Star's* office building. His assailants pursued him in their own car, following him into the lobby of his own building.

The negro chauffeur of the *Star's* editor, H. J. Haskell, was kidnapped in the Haskell car. He was driven to an alley where he was viciously beaten. He was shot at four times, but escaped with his life by breaking and running through side yards and alleys. What was the crime of the chauffeur? He had been caught in the reprehensible act of driving a Fusionist worker to the polls!

The machine's strong-arm boys got a little confused that day. Mistakes were bound to happen. In one mix-up they inadvertently killed one of their own precinct captains. James Lindley, a negro, had been working actively for the Fusionist ticket. On Sunday night before the election he was taken to Police Headquarters by one Bush Wells, a negro policeman, where he was booked for "investigation." Lindley was freed late Monday night on a writ of *habeas corpus.* On Tuesday he was working at the polling place in his ward, as he had every right to do. In the same polling place was one William Finley, a machine precinct captain. During the day, Bush Wells, the policeman mentioned above, happened to be driving in front of this polling place. He got out of the car, sauntered over to the desk in the polling place and told Lindley that he was needed "up the street for a few minutes." Finley, the precinct captain, said jokingly to Wells, "You oughtn't to take that man away. He's a good man." Wells walked off. Almost exactly three minutes later a car containing six men drove up in front of the polling place and went in. Lindley took one glance, and fled through the back door. One of the intruders, the leader, grabbed the first negro in sight, who happened to be a machine worker. Finley came to the aid of his associate and drew a gun. The intruders shot and killed him before he had a chance to pull the trigger of his own weapon. Here was a killing that resulted from what the people in the neighborhood insisted was a case of mistaken identity.

Lee Flacy, a newly married deputy sheriff, and a very popular young man, was on duty that day. He stopped in a café for a bite to eat. Thugs came in and intimidated him. They let him know that they considered his work that day a little too conscientious. The machine had no use for an officer harboring old-fashioned ideas of law and order. To emphasize their dislike for him they shot him in the leg and ran. Flacy dragged himself from the café and fired at his fleeing assailants. He wounded one of them, who later died. Another car suddenly appeared on the scene and opened fire on young Flacy, killing him instantly. One of their stray shots struck P. W. Oldham, a hardware merchant, who was just in the act of turning the key in the door to his shop. What an indictment of the

Pendergast machine! Even some of his henchmen on the City Council, who were accustomed to the rough and tumble of ward politics, were shocked at the needless bloodshed of this disgraceful municipal election of 1934.

A word from Pendergast would have prevented the criminal acts of that sanguinary election day. A fearless police director could have maintained order. A Fusionist delegation went to police headquarters early that day and asked for protection. Director of Police Eugene Reppert, refused them an audience. Later he told them, "You're getting protection," but he said it in a listless and cynical way. What could one expect of a police chief who counted among his friends and advisers such disreputable characters as Johnny Lazia, kingpin of the Kansas City underworld? Violence continued throughout the day, grew worse. The police gave no protection. Finally the desperate citizens telegraphed the Governor of Missouri and told him that law and order had collapsed completely and requested that he take immediate action. This message might as well have been directed to the planet Mars for all the relief it brought. "Uncle Tom's Cabin" (the capitol at Jefferson City) was closed that day, at least as far as helping the opponents of "Boss Tom" was concerned. The naïveté of the Fusionists!

Who won the "Bloody Election" of 1934? The newspaper headline the next morning read: "A Divided Machine in its Biggest Victory." And the vote? Out of a total registration of 244,000 a mere 222,866 votes were cast! Never let it be said that the people of Kansas City did not take the election of their city officials seriously.

The Pendergast candidate for Mayor won by 59,368 votes. In the Presidential Election of 1932 the Kansas City voters cast but 219,000 votes!

Let us move on to the year 1936.

"In the August, 1936, primary, Lawrence McDaniel, well-known St. Louis lawyer, was running for the State Supreme Court against Judge Ernest S. Gantt, a Pendergast machine candidate. McDaniel carried a substantial majority of the 114 counties in Missouri and the City of St. Louis, and, not counting Kansas City, he had a comfortable lead. Here's what became of him there. In the First Ward Gantt got 18,919 votes to eighteen for McDaniel—a ratio of 1,045 to one. In the Second Ward Gantt got 19,201 votes to thirteen for McDaniel, a ratio of 1,469 to one. In the last presidential election a vote of 41,805 was cast by the 38,401 babies, children and adults of these two wards!"[1]

I mentioned Pendergast's arithmetic at the beginning of this chapter. My aides and I began to take an interest in it. We got out pencil and paper and did some figuring of our own. Our answers did not check with Tom's. The Kansas City *Star* also became intrigued with Pendergast's mathematical wizardry. In 1936, preceding the election, it sent newsmen and photographers into the various wards to collect documentary evidence of irregularities in the registrations. Sensational and startling evidence was uncovered. Addresses of residences housing from ten to thirty registrants, according to the election board records, turned out to be vacant lots, or filling stations. Dwellings

[1] Ralph Coghlan, "Boss Pendergast," *Forum and Century,* February, 1937.

accommodating from three to five persons were padded with ten or fifteen "phantom" voters as shown by the evidence gathered by the *Star's* investigators. These findings were heralded daily in the outraged press and affidavits were gathered by a Citizens Committee. These incriminating facts were called to the attention of the Governor of Missouri and to the election commissioners of Kansas City.

Nothing was done, although the election board made a half-hearted attempt to purge the registration lists. But when a name was stricken from the list in one ward it turned up on the list in another ward, often by court order. On that election day in November, 1936, some 60,000 "ghost" voters stalked through the various polling places. The Pendergast forces won a landslide victory.

Evidence showed that this padded registration was due in large part to "repeaters" who went from one precinct to another, registering under false names, often as many as twenty or thirty times. Hordes of underworld characters flooded the polling places. It is surprising that the decent people of Kansas City took the trouble to vote at all. It was a foregone conclusion that any honest vote would be more than offset by "ghost" votes.

Two or three weeks prior to election day in 1936, armed with the accumulated evidence gathered through an investigation, members of the Citizens Committee called upon U.S. District Judge Merrill E. Otis and asked that a grand jury be called to delve more deeply into the situation. Judge Otis advised them to turn such evidence as they had over to the U.S. District Attorney's office. He said that he would confer with that office before coming to any decision in regard to calling a grand jury.

As the U.S. District Attorney at that time, I held a meeting in my office with delegated members of the Citizens Committee. It should be remembered that all this took place weeks before the election, not one vote had been cast, yet the committee was asking the Government to step in and call a grand jury. I knew without delving very far into the law books that the Committee's request was premature, for although the padding of the registration lists violated State laws, there was as yet no Federal statute violated. Our office simply had no jurisdiction until an election was held or a Federal statute violated.

I met with the Federal judges shortly thereafter and gave the opinion of my office on the technicalities involved. The judges were as well informed on the matter as I was, and they agreed that no action should be taken until after the election. All of us knew that more than small fry were involved, and we wanted to be on solid legal grounds when we put the Government machinery into action.

The 1936 election came and went without a repetition of the bloody episodes of 1934. On the surface everything seemed calm and orderly. One heard no open charges of corruption of the ballot, but a review of the election returns offered indisputable evidence of such corruption. These returns showed in many instances that all candidates on one party ticket received only two or three votes while the opposing candidates received six or seven hundred votes. We knew that no candidate was that popular. In one or two precincts the candidates for office on one party ticket received no votes whatsoever, even though the polls were manned by judges and clerks who represented evenly the Republican and Democratic parties. Another odd fact reflected by these certified election returns was that in numerous instances all candidates from Constable to President of the United States received exactly the same number of votes. This was too much of a coincidence. Things like this convinced us that the election reeked with corruption.

With this conviction strong in our minds we set about to examine the laws to determine whether a Federal statute had been violated and whether we had any jurisdiction to prosecute. Our first attempts to find a covering statute were fruitless. We discussed every remote possibility. Finally we came up with a statute which seemed to apply to the situation. This statute was enacted shortly after the Civil War and became known as the Civil Rights Statute. Law terms are boring to the layman, but since the statute above played such an important part in the breaking up of the Pendergast machine I think it should be cited. It is *Section 19* of the *Criminal Code* (*Section 5508 R.S. 18 U.S.C.A. 51*) and reads as follows:

> "If two or more persons conspire to injure, oppress, threaten, or intimidate any citizen in the free exercise or enjoyment of any right or privilege secured to him by the Constitution or laws of the United States, or because of his having exercised the same * * * they shall be fined not more than $5000 and imprisoned not more than ten years * * *"

This statute is brief in wordage and is rather mild in appearance, yet it covers a lot of territory and packs a real wallop as will be attested to by all those who have had any personal entanglement with its provisions.

Feeling that we were upon safe ground, we advised in writing the Honorable Albert L. Reeves, United States District Judge (whose turn it was to empanel the jury) of our conclusions on the legal questions involved, and he ordered a grand jury to be empaneled on December 14, 1936.

Early in my term of office I had experienced a rather unusual situation in a jury panel selected to try a prominent and politically influential citizen of Kansas City. The panel called upon that occasion was selected from one of the divisions of the Western District of Missouri. Of this panel a large number of prospective jurors were from Kansas City and Jackson County. We learned from a checkup that many of the men on this panel were city employees and political workers belonging to the same party organization as the defendant. Now since the vote fraud investigation was to concern Kansas City and Jackson County, we were pretty sure that disaster would accompany our efforts if the jury panel was selected from this division alone.

I called the judges' attention to a statute which authorizes the court to order juries to be drawn from any part of the district without assigning reasons therefor. The decisions of the Federal courts construing this statute in various cases had held that the statute applied to both grand and petit juries and that the court could exclude any county from the call. All summonses for jurors, both the grand jury and the trial jury, during the investigation and prosecution of vote frauds, were directed to the whole of the Western District of Missouri, comprising sixty-six counties, except that Kansas City and Jackson County were excluded by the order of the court. This was a severe blow to the Pendergast forces. It meant that they could not "pack" the jury.

On the morning of December 14, 1936, without previous warning to the public of the impending charge, a gray-haired veteran of the Federal courts, with a grim and determined countenance, mounted the bench. In a quiet, unpretentious court room this solemn-faced jurist began his charge to the jury. He soon warmed to his subject and in clarion tones that rang over the whole nation he courageously denounced corruption of the ballot in a manner never before witnessed in a Federal court room. Judge Reeves' charge to the Grand Jury received wide publicity, not only in Missouri but throughout the United States, and it was apparent to all that it rocked Kansas City from the lowest layer of its underworld to the highest stratum of its society.

"Gentlemen," said Judge Reeves, "there is crying need for the purification of the ballot in America. I can't sit quietly in my district, charged as I am with responsibility, and witness some man going with corrupt dripping fingers to the ballot box. A corrupt vote may be likened to a loaded and cocked gun pointed at the very heart of America. These conditions shame Kansas City. You have a wide range of inquiry. Don't stop until you have reached the uttermost parts of the city and into the ballot boxes of all districts to stop corruption of the ballot in this District. Gentlemen, reach for all, even if you find them in high authority. Move on them!"

That evening the Kansas City *Star* shattered its conservative habit of using one-column heads and broke out with a three-column bold-faced headline applauding the courage of Judge Reeves. It was as though the judge had shouted "Pendergast!" The implications of his directions to the Grand Jury were not lost upon the people of Kansas City, but there was a certain amount of skepticism. There was a widespread feeling that there was not a jury in Kansas City the Pendergast machine could not "fix." It would take more than an impassioned speech to a jury to clean the Augean stables of Kansas City. T. J. Pendergast was in New York when the blow fell, and when interviewed by reporters there said: "I have been investigated for forty years. If Reeves and Milligan can find anything wrong I'll not squawk."

Little did the Federal judges or my office realize that this investigation so gallantly launched would continue for a period of two years, that it would be waged not only in the District Court but in the United States Circuit Court of Appeals and finally in the United States Supreme Court itself. Prior to calling the Grand Jury we had determined that the ballots themselves would be the most vital evidence if we planned to carry on a successful prosecution. Therefore, the sound of Judge Reeves' voice had scarcely died away before the United States Marshal, acting upon detailed instructions and armed with *subpoenas duces tecum,* served upon all members of the Election Board the writs to produce before the Grand Jury forthwith all books, ballots, records, ballot boxes, and other election paraphernalia in their custody.

A few hours later I was visited by members of the

Election Board, who protested that it would take two or three days to deliver the ballots and records to the Marshal. I replied that I was sorry to hear that, as the subpoenas said nothing about "two or three days," but commanded that the ballots be delivered immediately, and that I was satisfied that if this was not done accordingly, the members of the Board would be in jail for contempt of court long before the "two or three days" were up. A rather significant incident occurred following the visit of the Election Board members to my office. One of them returned and said to me, "I am glad you said what you did. There are some very desperate men in this city, and if you don't get those ballots right away they will be destroyed, even if they have to burn the Court House down to get it done. I don't want to be responsible for the safety of those ballots."

By eight o'clock that night, truck loads of ballots and records weighing approximately twelve tons, had been received and at noon the following day all the election machinery had been impounded and was safe in the vaults of the Federal Building, under the control of the U. S. Marshal, Henry L. Dillingham, and remained there during the entire investigation.

Experts from the Federal Bureau of Investigation were called in to assist in examining the ballots. Ballots sealed in sacks were carried into the Grand Jury room and the first one opened contained positive proof that 95 ballots had been changed from straight Republican votes to straight Democratic votes. Ninety-five citizens of that small precinct had been deprived of their rights under the laws and the Constitution of the United States to have their votes counted as cast. Judges and clerks were made defendants in the indictments. Precinct captains, challengers, ward bosses and committeemen and women of both parties, and in a number of instances, police officers who were ostensibly the guardians of the polling places, were subjected to indictment.

In the early part of January, 1937, the jury made its first report to the court, returning three indictments involving twenty persons on charges of conspiracy under that Federal statute. The perpetrator of this great fraud, the Pendergast Democratic Organization, immediately sprang into action, and word was passed along the line that attorneys and bonds would be furnished free of charge to all defendants who were indicted. It was a typical Pendergast gesture of power, proving, if nothing else, that the Government's blow had struck home.

Following this first report of the Grand Jury the legal battle began. Corps of able lawyers rushed into the breach, arranged bond and immediately set in motion legal machinery intended to prevent the trials of those accused. My office did not for a moment underestimate the skill and resourcefulness of the formidable legal talent arrayed against us when the opening skirmishes of the battle were fought. That it was a fight to the finish soon became evident.

Pleas in abatement, demurrers and motions to quash the indictments were filed and argued before Judge Merrill E. Otis of the District Court. The most severe attacks were made upon the manner and substance of Judge Reeves' eloquent charge to the Grand Jury, previously referred to in this chapter. Defense counsel asserted in the most vigorous terms that the charge was "intemperate, inflammatory, argumentative, prejudicial, impassioned and designed, calculated to inflame and excite the passions and prejudices of the Grand Jury against the defendants and other election officials." Our opponents said that this was a direction to the Grand Jury to indict the defendants; that it was an abuse of judicial discretion and constituted a usurpation by the court of the functions of the Grand Jury; that it deprived the defendants of their right to an impartial hearing and was an expression of the guilt of the persons involved. They even went so far as to protest that the constitutional rights of the defendants had been violated.

Failing in their efforts to prevent trials of these defendants in the District Courts, their counsel sought relief in the United States Circuit Court of Appeals by an action filed in equity attempting to enjoin the United States Attorney's Office from prosecuting these cases in the District Courts. Two such attempts were made; both failed.

The strategy my office adopted was briefly as follows: to have the sealed sacks of ballots as received from the Election Board taken into the Grand Jury room, along with the records and other election paraphernalia; to have these sacks opened and the contents studied by the Grand Jury for alterations, changes or erasures. A powerful microscope was employed in the examination of the ballots. The poll books containing the names and addresses of voters, as well as the tabulation sheets of votes cast, were also carefully studied. At the conclusion of the examination of ballots from a given precinct they were separated and counted.

If in this detailed examination of ballots and records it was discovered that alterations or irregularities had occurred in a manner reflecting fraud or corruption, we immediately requested the FBI to procure written statements from each judge and clerk of the election district as to whether or not they thought the election procedure in said district was regular or irregular. Such statements were obtained relating to all matters that happened in the voting places during the process of election or the tabulation of returns that were made up for the Election Board, because we realized their value as evidence. The wisdom of this procedure was clearly demonstrated during the many trials that followed.

The next step was to call each judge and clerk before the Grand Jury. He was interviewed relative to all the events transpiring in the polling place during the casting, tabulation and certifying of votes. These interviews were then compared with the statements given to the FBI agents to discover discrepancies. Many a defendant was convicted by his own words.

Under the law governing elections in municipalities the size of Kansas City, the election officials are not permitted to open the ballot boxes or to count the votes until all the voters have voted and the polls have been closed. The law also requires that the voter's name and address must be written on consecutive numbered lines in the poll books as the voter appears and marks his ballot. These numbers run from one to one thousand for each precinct. The number at the beginning of the line on which the voter's name and address is written is also placed on the back of the ballot by the election judges. This enabled each individual ballot to be identified as belonging to a particular voter. The ballots also bear a serial number which is consecutive in the order of their printing. When a voter appears and asks for his ballot he gives the name and address to two judges who distribute the ballots and who are known as "Distributing Judges." The name of the voter is then checked against the registration book to determine if he is a legally qualified voter in that precinct.

In many instances it was found that a voter's ballot had been changed or altered in some way. We compared the number on the back of the ballot with that shown on the poll book. We found out in this way the name and address of the voter and summoned the voter whose ballot had been altered or changed. The voters were asked to identify the ballot they had voted and make a declaration as to the casting of the ballot for each candidate.

Following our plan of action, the original ballots and records were turned over to Charles Appel, Jr., expert examiner of the Federal Bureau of Investigation, who had established a laboratory for that purpose in Kansas City. He began a technical examination of the ballots and records. He photographed and enlarged questionable ballots, studied the fingerprints on them, and made all the necessary tests to determine if irregularities were indicated. He later revealed his findings in the trials.

These trials were followed with keen interest throughout the whole State. Citizens long accustomed to the highhanded methods of the Pendergast machine rejoiced as vote fraud conviction after vote fraud conviction made the "Boss" and his satellites squirm. The Kansas City *Star* and the St. Louis papers were quick to catch the significance of the Government's bold bid to strike at the very heart of the machine's power—the ballot box. The cartoonist Fitzpatrick, in the St. Louis *Post-Dispatch* even employed the box score device to depict Pendergast's losing battle. The famous Fitzpatrick was never more devastating than in these Kansas City vote fraud cartoons.

Arthur Krock wrote in *The New York Times*: "No great amount of outside attention appears to have been directed toward the valiant purge that is now being effected in the political corporation of Kansas City. Nevertheless, what a vigorous Federal District Attorney, a firm Federal Judge and some determined juries are doing to put fear into the ranks of the ruthless Pendergast machine is worth national notice and congratulation." I would like to point out that we had not laid a finger on Pendergast up to this point, but the enlightened press of the country was already linking his name with the vote fraud investigation. Legal technicalities which kept the name of Pendergast off our lips did not restrain the press.

Those who use the word "fraud" must produce proof. We had more proof than we needed. One of the most striking incidents of arrogant disregard of the rights of American citizens was the Grand Jury's discovery that in one precinct not one ballot was ever viewed with the intention of counting it by any judge or clerk of that polling place. There was conclusive evidence that the ballots had never been unfolded for the purpose of counting them. Those ballots had been dumped from the ballot box into the sack which was sealed and delivered to the office of the Election Commissioners without even a routine count by the election officials.

Another incident which reveals the highhanded method by which the rights of voters were disregarded occurred in a precinct in a certain Kansas City ward notorious for the registration of "ghost pads." The Missouri election laws require, as heretofore stated, that the polls be kept open in cities the size of Kansas City until seven o'clock in the evening. In this particular precinct, at 4:30 in the afternoon a precinct captain, who was not even an election official and had no lawful right in the polling place, ran the hands of the clock up to 7:00 P.M., went to the doors of the polling place and blandly announced that the polls were closed. Voters who were still waiting to cast their vote protested vigorously to the authorities but the polling place remained closed. Instead of counting the ballots, that precinct captain read from a memorandum which he held in his hand the number of votes arbitrarily allotted to the Democratic candidates and the number conceded to their Republican opponents. The several election officials signed the certification making affidavit to the accuracy of their count and the ballots were delivered to the Election Commissioners.

A respectable housewife in one precinct was told that she would be "taken for a ride" if she did not obey the command of the precinct captain to put her signature on the certification of false election returns. She signed under duress. In another precinct an election official, a frail and elderly man, insisted upon making an honest count of the votes cast. He was bodily ejected from the polling place by three gangsters who were stationed in the neighborhood for the express purpose of intimidating voters and election officials who might be so bold as to protest any irregularities. Johnny Lazia was dead, but his spirit went marching on!

Testimony clearly revealed that on the day before the election of 1936 there were at least 50,000 fictitious names on the registration books of Kansas City—phantom names of people who did not exist or who were not qualified voters. These false names were known by the underworld as "Pads," "Spooks," "Ghosts," "Sleepers," or "Riders." Vote frauds are the rule rather than the exception in a city where the thugs actually differentiate between the types of false names on the registration books! An argot like this does not develop overnight. Lexicographers please note.

So particular were these "ballotsmiths" that they were offended when the slang terms were misused. For instance, there were fine shades of connotation in the words "Pads," "Sleepers," "Spooks," and "Riders." The brigands of the ballot box used "Spooks" and "Ghosts" only in reference to the names of ethereal visitors from that "bourne from whence no traveler returns," or, to put it another way, "cemetery commuters." The raising of the dead around election day was something marvelous to behold. "Sleepers" seemed to denote persons who at one time may have lived in the precinct but who had moved elsewhere, yet still had their names on the registration lists. "Riders" referred neither to cowboys or Klansmen. According to the best available information this designation was applied to a host of vote stealers who, on registration day or election day, rode the range of the precincts leaving their brand on the registration books in every political corral. "Pad" is the generic term including all of the various brands that were herded together during the general round-up on election day. Appropriate terms for a cattle town.

The first trial opened on a bleak morning in February. Unfriendly winds swept the city streets, driving occasional gusts of snow before them. Shortly after dawn the crowds had already gathered in front of the Federal Building. Groups of interested lawyers elbowed their way through the wise-cracking crowds that thronged the hallways. When the doors of the courtroom were thrown open the crowd surged in, filling the place to overflowing. The radio broadcasting systems had installed loud speakers. The defendants sat grouped around the defense table. Members of the press leaned forward expectantly with pencils poised. Serious-faced jurors, summonsed for the trial, men from various walks of life, filed silently in and seated themselves in the jury box. The court reporters, with professional poise and efficiency, took their place before the witness stand. The Clerk of the Court seated himself at the foot of the judge's bench. Representatives of the Government sat down at the table assigned to the prosecution. A gavel was raised, held aloft. The door of the judge's chamber opened. The audience arose. The gavel sounded, the judge mounted the bench, the bailiff proclaimed the opening of court and the drama began to unfold. It held the stage for two years.

The battle was hard fought. Defense counsel raised objections at every point. Bit by bit we drew from the witnesses the evidence which exposed the fraud and corruption of the 1936 election. The cumulative effect of all this mounting pile of documented facts shocked the sensibilities of honest jurors and citizens who were listening in or following the accounts of the trials in the newspapers. Even the hard-boiled reporters of the various papers were amazed at some of the hitherto undisclosed ramifications of the gigantic steal perpetrated by the Pendergast pirates. In spite of all this there were some men who refused to admit that there was anything sinister about the Pendergast machine. The then Senator Harry S. Truman, trying to block my reappointment as U. S. District Attorney while I was in the very midst of the vote fraud trials, said: "I say to the Senate, Mr. President, that a Jackson County, Mo., Democrat has as much chance of a fair trial in the Federal District Court of Western Missouri as a Jew would have in a Hitler court or a Trotsky follower before Stalin. Indictments have been wholesale. Convictions have been a foregone conclusion. Verdicts have been directed." [1]

The St. Louis *Globe Democrat* in an editorial entitled: "Truman Exposes Himself," made this observation: "Judges Reeves and Otis are neither Hitlers nor Stalins. Occasionally, however, as in Kansas City, we need Judges

[1] *Congressional Record,* Feb. 15, 1938.

who are not afraid of political machines or political bosses."[1]

Before going on with my description of the courtroom scenes and some of the more shocking revelations of the various trials I want to take time out to put the reader straight on a matter or two that the Truman quotation brings to my mind. When the then Senator made his remarks about the vote fraud cases and Federal justice in Western Missouri my reply to inquiring reporters was, "No comment." Judge Reeves was more outspoken. He said the Truman outburst in the Senate was "a speech of a man nominated by 'ghost' votes, elected with 'ghost' votes and whose speech was probably written by 'ghost' writers."[2] If there were any Hitler methods being used in Kansas City at that time I know pretty well who was employing them, and perhaps in the next paragraph or two the reader will know, too.

Shortly after Judge Reeves charged the Grand Jury to investigate the election of 1936, the machine not only directed its attorneys to use every available legal process to halt and hamper the progress of the investigation and trials, but through its underworld connections began a series of intimidations directed mainly at the two Federal judges and their families. Nights were rendered sleepless by constant telephone calls conveying threats and intimations of violence. The wives of the jurists were annoyed and frightened throughout the day by telephone calls from unknown women who made base insinuations of a

[1] St. Louis *Globe Democrat*, Feb. 17, 1938.
[2] Kansas City *Star*, Feb. 15, 1938.

defamatory character against the jurists. One judge received a call every hour on the hour and a sinister voice predicted dire revenge if the investigations were not halted. This "Gestapo" method became so frightful that the judges were obliged to have their telephone numbers changed to secret or silent numbers.

A diabolical attempt was made to "frame" one of the judges on an occasion when he was holding court in another city in the district. As usual in this kind of blackmail setting, the familiar bait, a woman and a camera, were to be used, but the judge was too wary to be led into such an obvious trap.

Residing at a local hotel during the week I was not subjected to the telephone technique employed on the judges, but I received a friendly word from an underworld source that I should "keep off the highways after sundown." This warning was rather pointed as it was my custom to drive to my old home in Richmond, some forty miles away, and remain there over the weekends. The wisdom of this tip was demonstrated shortly thereafter when a serious attempt was made to crowd my brother's car off the highway and into a ditch. This incident, we decided, was merely a case of mistaken identity since my brother closely resembles me.

From my friends I received advice and warnings to watch my step. I listened attentively to this advice, but feeling all the while if something was to happen to me there was little I could do to prevent it. However, I did not permit this fatalistic viewpoint to completely govern my actions. I confined my night life in the city to an occasional movie, attending the early showing and not the advertised midnight show. A friendly veteran of the FBI persuaded me, without too much effort, to keep on the night table of my hotel apartment his vicious-looking 45 caliber revolver. This "protector" kept me company during the years of my investigations. During my weekly visits to Richmond I took the precaution of keeping the shades drawn at night, and placing on the windows and doors of my white frame garage little white strips of adhesive tape so that I might know if the garage had been entered and my car tampered with during the night.

To return to the vote fraud trials. The jury and audience listened with consternation as the story of the spoliation of the franchise was revealed. The victims of the ruthless system which had held Kansas City writhing in its grasp for so many years paraded before the bar of justice. One little old lady told in a feeble voice of an experience as pathetic as it was infuriating. Desiring to perform her duty as a citizen for the last time she was taken by her family to the polling place. With the wisdom that comes with eighty years she gave expression to her views regarding the sanctity of the ballot. The jurors cast kindly glances in her direction, and their faces clouded up when she told how ruffians had denied her the opportunity to cast her vote. She had gone to the polls at the peril of her health, and had been humiliated and rebuffed by hoodlums in the pay of corrupt Pendergast henchmen.

The defense witnesses had their day in court. Brilliant lawyers drew from their star witnesses statements designed to throw an aura of credibility around charges and countercharges flung from the defense table. The jurors had to wrestle with contradictory statements. Under the blessings of our system of government a man is deemed innocent until proved guilty. The Government knew that truth would prevail in the end, but it was not enough for us to cry "fraud." Our evidence had to be produced bit by bit.

Slowly and with infinite care the Government concluded its case. All the evidence was in and the jury retired. The die was cast.

There were many dramatic moments in that interval of time during which the jury was behind locked doors trying to arrive at a true verdict. The lawyers on both sides were nervous and hopeful. Nothing any of them could say now would have any influence on the jury. A haze of tobacco smoke filled the waiting courtroom. The usual coughing and clearing of throats was heard. Newspapermen wandered from table to table requesting statements of one kind or another, anything to add human interest and color to their stories. Suspense mounted.

Finally the word was whispered around that the jury had completed its deliberations and that a verdict was forthcoming. A hush fell over the audience. Those who have experienced this zero hour can never forget it. The jury filed in. The foreman handed the written verdict to the clerk. In stentorian tones he read: ". . . GUILTY AS CHARGED . . ." The suspense was over. The Government had won another case. Another brick was removed from the imposing Pendergast edifice. Sooner or later we would find the keystone of the arch—then the whole building would collapse.

And so rang down the curtain on a drama enacted in

thirteen successive trials in which not one defendant was acquitted. Each of these sensational trials was characterized by its own peculiar kind of fraud and chicanery. Each revealed a new and startling method of defrauding the voters. The most incriminating factor in all of these trials was the display before the eyes of the jurors of the corrupted ballots themselves. These mute witnesses spoke more eloquently than words. Alibis were of no avail in the face of these documents.

We discovered some odd facts in looking into the frauds of the 1936 election in Kansas City. A barber shop served as a polling place in one precinct. At the proper moment the "ballotsmiths" took the box of ballots down into the basement, dumped its contents on a table and began to study them. They were afraid some of the unintelligent voters had not marked their ballots properly and such slight inaccuracies ought to be corrected. To their utter dismay they found that 113 voters had absent-mindedly voted for Republican candidates! This was annoying, for it meant that all these Republican ballots had to be erased and Democratic ballots substituted. After it was all over one of the officials went upstairs and reclined in an empty barber chair. "I am all in," he told a friend. "Some of those damned Republicans marked their ballots so hard it was all I could do to rub them out."

Another polling place was in a display room of the Kansas City Monument Company. One of the women judges at this place let it be known that she was honest —a *faux pas* in Pendergastian society—and a more sociable judge was soon found. "We jerked the old girl out and put in one of our own men," the precinct captain boasted.

In this polling place the officials nonchalantly dumped the ballots on a convenient tombstone and erased Republican names and wrote in the names of deserving Democrats. Still 150 names short of the quota, the officials drew out a list of "ghost" names, had them certified and the shortage was miraculously remedied. "We have everyone fixed from the Governor down," one official reassured a timid woman who remonstrated against such highhanded methods.

In one old-fashioned neighborhood the polling place was in the Sunday School room of a little church. The receiving judge lifted ballots from the box, slipped them unseen to his associate, who retired to the sacred silence of the church where he spread the ballots out in the pulpit and changed them to suit the known wishes of the Pendergast machine.

Why go on at the risk of boring the surfeited reader? If anything I have written sounds fantastic or exaggerated please bear in mind that all these incidents and hundreds of others are preserved in the court records. They would fill many books the size of this one. A total of 39 indictments was returned, involving 278 defendants. Many were women. Of these 278 defendants, 259 were convicted; 19 were dismissed for one reason or another, but one challenging fact stands out above all others. Not one defendant was acquitted by the judge or the juries. This could hardly be, as the then Senator Truman would have had us believe, a "persecution" of innocent men and women. The evidence of fraud was so voluminous, so flagrant, so overwhelming, that anything but a verdict of "Guilty as charged" would have been a miscarriage of justice.

V

SMASH UP!

The Insurance Scandal

THIS is the story of an insurance scandal and its aftermath. It names names and cites figures. It is a true account of how the Federal Government closed in on Pendergast and rocked his political machine to its foundations.

The Government built up its case piece by piece. There seems no other way of recording the events in this chapter except piece by piece.

When this chronicle opens, the State of Missouri had been engaged for some time in litigation with fire insurance companies doing business in the state, over the matter of rates charged policy holders. Early in the 1920's, Insurance Commissioner Hyde of Missouri attempted to effect a saving to policy holders by a blanket reduction of premium rates. The companies involved bitterly contested this effort and waged an unsuccessful battle through the courts of Missouri to the highest court of the land, but in the end the policy owners won out, thanks to the firm and courageous action of the Commissioner.

The issue of rates arose again on December 30, 1929. This time the insurance companies began new litigation by serving notice on the then Superintendent of Insurance, Joseph B. Thompson, that fire insurance would be increased 16 2/3 per cent in Missouri. The Superintendent of Insurance promptly refused to allow the increase to become effective. Notwithstanding, the companies proceeded to collect from their policy holders the 16 2/3 per cent increase in the premium rate and immediately sought by legal proceedings in the State Court and in the United States District Court, to enjoin and prohibit the Superintendent of Insurance from interference with the collection of same. Pending the outcome of that litigation, these courts ordered that the 16 2/3 per cent excess premiums thus collected by the fire insurance companies be impounded.

By 1935, the impounded premiums in the Federal Court alone amounted to more than $9,000,000. On May 18, 1935, Robert Emmett O'Malley, who, at the instance of Thomas J. Pendergast, had been appointed to the office of Superintendent of Insurance by Governor Guy B. Park in 1933, signed a so-called compromise agreement with the agent for the fire insurance companies, Charles R. Street, by which it was agreed that the fire insurance rate litigation should be ended and that the impounded premiums in both courts should be divided so that the fire insurance companies would receive 80% of the premiums and the policy holders only 20%. Subsequently, the so-called compromise was taken under advisement by the court.

On February 1, 1936, the court approved the settlement and entered its order that the impounded premiums be distributed by the custodian in accordance with the provisions of the written agreement; namely, 20% payable at once to the policy holders, 50% payable at once to the fire insurance companies, and 30% payable into a trust fund of which Charles R. Street and Robert J. Felonie were the trustees, the former being the representative of the insurance companies and the latter their chief legal counsel. Out of the trust fund they were ordered, pursuant to the terms of the agreement, to pay first the expenses of the litigation and then to pay the balance of the fund to the insurance companies. On that eventful day in February, 1936, there was rung down the curtain on more than twelve years of litigation over fire insurance rates, and, according to the records, the books were closed.

For two years following the settlement of the insurance cases, more than vague rumors had disturbed the surface of the placid insurance waters in Missouri. Early in 1938 a former Missourian, who had served many years under the Commissioner of Internal Revenue in Washington, decided to leave the Government service and engage in private business in New York. Before leaving Washington this honest and courageous official revealed to an enterprising Washington correspondent of the Kansas City *Star* a most startling and interesting story relative to the insurance litigation in his native state. He said that in April, 1936, agents of the Internal Revenue office in Chicago, in checking the income tax returns of the law firm of Hicks and Felonie, chief counsel of the fire insurance companies involved in the Missouri litigation, had uncovered definite proof that fourteen checks, made payable to the law firm and signed by fourteen different large insurance companies, and totaling the sum of

$100,500, had been passed on to Charles R. Street, vice-president of the General American Insurance Company. This was the same individual who had been in charge of the litigation as representative of the insurance companies, and who had manipulated the compromise settlement. He further related that agents of the U.S. Treasury had called upon Mr. Street, and upon being questioned Street admitted that he had received $100,500 from the insurance companies via the firm of Hicks and Felonie, but stated that he had disbursed the money to someone else, and that it did not represent money belonging to him. Upon being asked to name the person to whom he gave the money he refused to furnish any information regarding the identity of such a person beyond a statement that the person was high in political circles in Missouri but not a public officer. The agents, of course, demanded that the identity of this person be revealed. Later Street advised the Bureau of Internal Revenue by letter that he could not identify the person to whom payment had been made until the liner "Queen Mary," then at sea on her maiden voyage, had docked at New York. The ship docked, but Street still did not reveal the name the agents sought. He did file an amended income tax return with the Internal Revenue Bureau, in effect retracting the statement he had paid the money to another person and stating that he himself had received and retained the same for his own use and had paid the additional tax and interest on such alleged income.

The *Star's* correspondent was further advised that the agents of the Bureau, after a brief inspection of the "Queen Mary's" passenger list on the historic voyage mentioned above found entered there the name of T. J. Pendergast, Missouri's most powerful politician. An unsuccessful effort was made to determine whether any part of the $100,500 disbursed by Street had reached Pendergast. That was the end of the former Government employee's story. Apparently for more than two years these facts remained locked in the vaults of the Bureau of Internal Revenue. No record, to my knowledge, exists of further investigation into subsequent financial machinations of Street and the insurance companies until this former government official brought to light the story above set forth.

The Kansas City *Star's* correspondent felt impelled by a sense of public duty to pass this information on to some authoritative person in Missouri. He went direct to Governor Lloyd Stark, who in turn advised me fully of the details of this revelation.

Soon thereafter I received a long distance telephone call from Washington. Governor Stark was on the wire and he urgently requested that I come immediately to Washington for a conference with the Treasury officials relative to this matter. Upon my arrival I was advised by Governor Stark that he had talked to President Roosevelt and told him the story of this insurance betrayal, and had urged on the President that the Treasury Department should institute a further and far-reaching investigation to ascertain whether or not additional payments of money had been made in what was obviously an insurance scandal. The President, he said, was genuinely interested and called Mr. Morgenthau to advise him that the Governor of Missouri would call upon him and place the facts before him, and that he wanted the Secretary of the Treasury to cooperate in every way to bring about a complete investigation. Governor Stark told me that a conference had been arranged in the old Treasury Building that night, and that I was to attend.

At the opening of the conference, with many officials of the Internal Revenue Department present, the Governor brought forth a small black memorandum book and began a factual review of the supposed file of the Bureau. He related that the file "contained photostatic copies of fourteen checks signed by fourteen different fire insurance companies made payable to Charles R. Street, in the total sum of $100,500"; that these checks had been traced through the firm of Hicks and Felonie; that the money was received by Street who had advised Treasury agents that he paid the money to a person in Missouri who was important politically but not an official.

I was amused at the expressions on the faces of the officials as the Governor unfolded the purported contents of the file. They seemed to be amazed at his knowledge of the contents of the department's own confidential file. At no time did the Governor volunteer a word as to the source of his information.

The spokesman for the group assured us that a further and more sweeping investigation would immediately be launched, and that Mr. Rudolph Hartmann, one of their best and most capable men of the Intelligence Unit, would be in charge and conduct the investigation. Following our conference the Intelligence Unit swung into action as promised, and began one of the most thorough and far-reaching investigations in the annals of income tax inquiries. I can personally attest to the capabilities of Mr. Hartmann by reason of my many months of association with him. He was a most colorful figure, six feet three inches tall, with strong regular features, thick black hair and dark brown eyes that seemed ever alert and seeking some hidden object. Of German extraction he possessed that type of scientific mind which catalogues facts carefully and effectively, overlooking no detail. It was mainly through his tireless efforts that every dollar of the $50,000 ransom paid in the celebrated Lindbergh kidnapping case was traced to the possession of the kidnapper and killer, Bruno Hauptmann—every dollar, except the sum of $40 which he was unable to trace, though he worked two long weeks in a futile effort to do so.

One important figure who might have helped us in this case, Charles R. Street, the man who collected the $100,500, died February 2, 1938, and thereby removed a voice which could have told us a sordid story of intrigue and scandal.

I kept in constant touch with Hartmann during the many months of inquiry. I learned that in the investigation of Street's affairs the investigators had accidentally stumbled upon the fact that Street kept, besides his own personal bank account, a special account, and that thorough examination of this account revealed that Street had collected an additional sum of $330,000 from the fire insurance companies and had disbursed same to some unknown person. In addition to this it was discovered that Street had paid A. L. McCormack of St. Louis, Missouri, two separate amounts of money, one $20,000 and the other payment $10,000.

This made it crystal clear that Street had received a total of $460,000 from the insurance companies engaged in the Missouri litigation, and it took little deduction to arrive at a definite conclusion that this money was paid to someone in the state. But we still had to prove the identity of that person.

McCormack's connection with Street received immediate attention. The Government agents interviewed him and made a careful investigation of his financial transactions. Inquiry revealed that McCormack was the president of an insurance agency in St. Louis and represented some seventeen fire insurance companies doing business in Missouri; that he had at one time during the litigation been elected president of the Missouri Fire Insurance Agents' Association, and that he had played an active role in the settlement of the litigation.

McCormack admitted that he received the two payments from Street, but claimed that this was for services rendered the insurance companies during the long years of litigation. He had failed to mention these payments in his income tax returns, but he later corrected this slight oversight by filing amended returns and paying the tax on this additional income. The Government sleuths turned McCormack's business accounts inside out but found no actual proof that any of this money had ever reached the pockets of any other person.

The investigators were convinced that the itching palm of Boss Pendergast was the ultimate destination of this almost fabulous sum of money, but they were unable to find the necessary evidence to substantiate the fact in a court of justice. The inquiry had reached an impasse and agent Hartmann requested a conference to discuss the situation. In his blunt, humorless, objective fashion he frankly related to me and my assistant the dilemma he and his investigators were in. They had traced $460,000 of the insurance money to Street, and $30,000 to McCormack, but from that point on they were stymied. "We can get no further," Hartmann said with finality. "It's up to you to break the case. Your office may be able to do it through a grand jury investigation."

Our conference broke up with the assurance that my office would call a grand jury and that McCormack would be handed a subpoena. We also secured from the agents the names and addresses of the chief executives of the largest fire insurance companies involved in the litigation and had subpoenas issued for them and the records of their companies.

When the morning arrived for the session of the Grand Jury, the Federal Building took on an unusual aspect. Among those present were the head officials of some of the most powerful insurance companies in America: B. M. Culver of the Continental Insurance Company, Robert R. Clark of the Caledonian Insurance Co., W. H. Koop and W. H. Redmayne of the Great American Insurance Co., Wilfred Kurth of the Home Insurance Company, George C. Long of the Phoenix Insurance Co. of Hartford, J. H. Vreeland of the Scottish Union and National Insurance Co., and Robert J. Felonie, chief counsel of the fire insurance companies.

To give the reader an inside picture of the breaking of the insurance scandal it becomes necessary for me to record the events leading up to it in a very personal manner. I invited the insurance executives into my private office and frankly informed them that it was our intention to learn the truth of this transaction. I stated that while I realized that they were all men of large business affairs, I was in no sense awed by their importance in the business world, and that I was determined to break the case one way or another, throwing in the hint that one of those methods would be very embarrassing to the group assembled.

I advised them that we had conclusive proof that Charles Street had collected at least $460,000 from the companies and that he had used this money in bringing about a settlement of the Missouri litigation. We now wanted an answer to the question, who got the money? The executives readily admitted that the money was raised by assessing the various companies doing business in Missouri (some 234 companies), and that Street had been intrusted with the funds for additional legal expenses, but denied emphatically that they had any knowledge of the fund being used to corrupt any official or in bringing about any illegal settlement of the case.

In the meantime, McCormack was taken at intervals before the Grand Jury in an effort to solve the mystery. For three long days the executives were my office guests. Not one of them was taken before the jury but daily I had sessions with the whole group or singly in an effort to get at the whole truth. On the third day we began taking an inventory of the situation and came to the conclusion that we had got exactly nowhere in our inquiry. In desperation I decided the time had come to adopt different tactics. I ceased to be the courteous, thoughtful District Attorney. At three o'clock I announced to the group that they had failed to cooperate with us and then stated that I was going to break the case in spite of their lack of cooperation, and that the method to be used would subject them to a good deal of embarrassment.

With the knowledge that McCormack had been in the insurance business for years in St. Louis and that he, at that time, represented as agent seventeen insurance companies, I said to the executives: "You men can put the heat on McCormack and make him tell the story. It's up to you! If you don't do this I will use my own method." I left them alone in the office following this ultimatum. In a very short time one of the group requested that they be excused, with the additional request that McCormack be allowed to leave the Federal Building. To these requests I readily assented.

During the night I received a telephone call at my hotel from one of the principal insurance officials stating that he wished to see me early in the morning. I replied that I would be at the office any time he suggested. He stated he wished to talk with me before I went to the office. I invited him to have early breakfast with me. After coffee was served he informed me that the officials had held a conference the night before with McCormack and that they had persuaded him to tell the whole story and that he had agreed to be at my office at 10:30 A.M. and make a complete revelation.

The receipt of this news was indeed most gratifying. McCormack's story would give us the evidence we needed to crack the case. I sat at my desk anxiously awaiting the arrival of McCormack, but I received a telephone call from his lawyer stating that McCormack had not been able to sleep during the night and requested that our conference be postponed until two o'clock. Promptly at that hour McCormack entered my office. He was alone. He sat down in a chair across the desk from me.

McCormack possessed a powerful physique. He was forty-eight years old, stood six feet two inches in height, and was well preserved. In his early days he had studied law and became a member of the bar in St. Louis preceding his entrance into the insurance business. During this investigation I had more than one lively tiff with him, which once or twice almost led to a personal encounter, but at a glance I saw that he apparently bore no malice toward me on that afternoon. I said in a friendly voice, "Mac, let's have the story." He immediately asked for a piece of paper and a pencil and began writing the items of amounts he had received from Street and details of payments made to Pendergast, the amounts paid to O'Malley at the Boss's suggestion and the amounts he retained for himself.

After McCormack began making his notes he stopped suddenly, and wadding the paper into a ball tossed it in the waste paper basket. I, thinking he had changed his mind, made a dive for the basket and retrieved the paper.

He had only made a slight error in the figures, but I was taking no chances of losing those precious figures which I knew could be used in evidence if he failed to tell the story.

McCormack said that on Sunday, January 13, 1935, Robert Emmett O'Malley, State Superintendent of Insurance, came to St. Louis and registered at the Coronado Hotel in rooms 925 and 926. In one of these rooms he and O'Malley held a conference. McCormack at the time was President of the Missouri Insurance Agents' Association and had been active in the litigation on behalf of Charles R. Street. O'Malley asked McCormack if he thought the insurance companies would like to settle the rate cases. He replied that he thought they would be very much interested in doing so. O'Malley then asked whether the companies would be willing to pay anybody helping them make such a settlement. McCormack replied that while he could not answer for the companies he believed that Charles R. Street, who was in Chicago, would be glad to receive any proposal and that he would place any suggestions before him. O'Malley said that any settlement would have to be arranged through T. J. Pendergast and that a meeting between Street and Pendergast might help a lot in settling the rate cases. McCormack stated that he would go to Street and acquaint him with this conversation. On the following day he made good his promise and went to Chicago to talk to Street.

At Chicago he told Street about O'Malley's suggestion that the settlement of the rate cases might be arranged to the advantage of the insurance companies if Street and

Pendergast could get together and talk things over. Street said that he would be delighted to discuss the matter with Pendergast, for he knew the insurance companies were very eager to have the long-drawn-out litigation settled. McCormack told me that at this conference with Street, no discussion of what amount of money would be necessary was entered into.

McCormack returned to St. Louis. Three days later O'Malley, the State Superintendent of Insurance, again came to St. Louis and registered at the Coronado Hotel, occupying the same rooms he had previously occupied, and remained there until January 21, 1935. McCormack stated that he visited O'Malley and discussed the insurance rate litigation once more, and told how enthusiastic Street had been over the prospect of a settlement; of his willingness to meet Pendergast in Chicago. O'Malley promised to report this to Pendergast, and suggested that McCormack see Street and have him set a date for Pendergast's visit to Chicago. On January 22, 1935, McCormack went to Chicago and told Street all that O'Malley had suggested. To make a long story short, Pendergast came to Chicago and registered at the Congress Hotel. McCormack was staying at the Palmer House, and he arranged for Pendergast and Street to meet in his rooms. Street opened the conference by relating the complete story of the insurance litigation and the serious set-backs suffered by the companies as a result, and hinted to Pendergast that the companies were anxious to settle provided they received a favorable settlement. Pendergast replied that he could convince the State officials that a settlement would be advisable. Street then bluntly asked Pendergast how much the "deal" would cost, and Pendergast told him to make an offer. Street offered $200,000, but Pendergast said he would not touch it at that figure. Street then raised the ante to $500,000, and Pendergast accepted.

McCormack paused a moment in his story as though sensing that what he had just said was of supreme interest to me. It was. I was getting a true picture of the shrewd, calculating boss gambling for big stakes.

He went on with his account of the big deal. He said that no mention was made at this time as to the manner in which the $500,000 was to be paid. Pendergast said he would take the matter of the insurance rate settlement up the moment he got back to Kansas City. "McCormack also could be of help in making the settlement," he said. While still in the room he called Kansas City by telephone and placed a bet on a horse. He offered to pay for the call.

On March 28, 1935, McCormack stated that he again went to Chicago and put up at the Stevens Hotel, room 2011-A. He met Street, and Street said that he believed Pendergast would exert more influence with State officials if he were offered more money. Pendergast was in Chicago at the time, so another meeting was arranged in McCormack's room, and this time Street told Pendergast that he was increasing the original offer to $750,000. Pendergast seemed pleased, and readily accepted the new offer.

On May 8, 1935, McCormack went to Chicago at Street's request. Street handed him $50,000 in currency and directed him to deliver it to Pendergast in Kansas City. McCormack took a plane and about two hours later landed at the Kansas City airport. He drove immediately to the Jackson County Democratic Club at 1908 Main Street, where Pendergast had his office. He handed the $50,000 to him, and Pendergast put it in a safe. This amount was part of the $100,500 shown by the partnership books of Hicks and Felonie to have passed out of Street's hands and through the partnership account and back into his hands on May 9, 1935.

McCormack went on to say that on May 14, 1935, six days later, a conference was held in the Muehlebach Hotel in Kansas City, Missouri, between Street and officials and attorneys for the fire insurance companies, and O'Malley, State Superintendent of Insurance, and attorneys representing the insurance department. On that day tentative plans for the settlement were made and representatives of the State and fire insurance companies made a written draft of tentative plans.

On May 18, 1935, four days after the conference at the Muehlebach, the tentative plans for the settlement were drafted into a written agreement signed by O'Malley and Street in their capacity as representatives, but not until O'Malley had taken the document to Pendergast for approval. On May 21, 1935, McCormack went to Chicago, met Street, and was handed an additional $50,000 in currency with instructions to deliver it to Pendergast. Once more McCormack boarded a plane and delivered the money to Pendergast in Kansas City. Pendergast took only $5,000 for himself on this occasion. He handed McCormack $45,000, with instructions that he give O'Malley $22,500 and to keep a like amount himself. Then Pendergast took McCormack to the Riverside race track for a bit of relaxation. This $50,000 payment was the last of the $100,500 shown by the partnership books of the firm of Hicks and Felonie to have passed through Street's hands, through the partnership account and back into his own. There now remained of the original amount which went through the partnership account only $500. Street kept this for himself. When McCormack returned to St. Louis he gave O'Malley the money Pendergast had requested him to deliver, and O'Malley asked him to retain it in his safe deposit box as he himself had no place to keep it. He said he would draw from it as he needed it. McCormack stated that he disbursed the entire sum of $22,500 to O'Malley in various amounts.

Subsequently, the so-called compromise and agreement executed by Street and O'Malley was presented to the court as a valid and untainted agreement and the court took it under advisement. On February 1, 1936, the court entered its order that the premiums impounded by the court be distributed by the custodian in accordance with the written agreement; namely, 20% payable at once to the policy holders, 50% payable at once to the fire insurance companies, and 30% payable into a trust fund of which Street and Felonie were trustees. Out of this trust fund the trustees were ordered first to pay the expenses of litigation, then to pay the balance to the fire insurance companies. After the payment of expenses there remained in this trust fund a sum equal to 16% of the total impounded premiums, a sum the insurance companies were entitled to receive. Each company did receive a payment representing 11% of its impounded premiums, but with this went a memorandum from Street directing them to issue their checks to him as their agent in an amount representing 5% of their total impounded premiums. This was done by each company. The total amount paid to Street by these checks was $330,000.

Late in March, 1936, Street sent word to McCormack to come to Chicago on April 11. On that day Street handed McCormack the $330,000 he had received from the insurance companies and told him to deliver same to Pendergast in Kansas City. McCormack put the money in a Gladstone bag, caught a train to Kansas City, and on arriving there took a taxi to the Pendergast mansion at 5650 Ward Parkway. Pendergast was expecting him. He took the money and carefully counted it. After the count was made Pendergast turned to McCormack and told him that he was keeping for himself only $250,000, and that he was returning $80,000, of which amount McCormack could keep $40,000 for himself and give the other $40,000 to O'Malley. McCormack delivered O'Malley his share a few days later in St. Louis.

By this time $430,000 of the agreed price of $750,000 had been delivered to Pendergast, and of that amount Pendergast had kept for himself $305,000. On October 20, 1936, O'Malley visited McCormack in St. Louis and told him that Pendergast was ill and had to have an operation and was in need of money. He said that he would appreciate it if McCormack would go to Chicago and ask Street for $10,000. This McCormack agreed to do, and in due time the money was obtained and McCormack delivered it in person to Menorah Hospital in Kansas City where Pendergast was recovering from an operation. So far a total of $440,000 had been paid to Pendergast by

Street, but before further payment could be made Street died, leaving a total unpaid balance of $310,000 due Pendergast.

This revelation has been tedious perhaps to readers who do not care for facts and figures, but it completely solved the insurance scandal and brought to light the machinations and intrigue employed in bringing about fraudulent settlement of years of litigation in the State and Federal Courts. It tore the mask from Thomas J. Pendergast, the "benevolent boss whose word was as good as his bond," revealing him in his true light, a cold, calculating corruptionist. It took only a casual glance at the income tax returns filed by Pendergast and O'Malley for the years 1935-36 to ascertain that not one penny of the insurance money received had been reported. This was clearly a case of income tax evasion, and the next move in this fast-moving drama was our feverish preparation of indictments to be presented to the Grand Jury. We were not concerned with the returns filed by McCormack since he was a resident of St. Louis, which was outside of our jurisdiction.

I advised the agent in charge of the investigation to prepare a résumé of the evidence uncovered and appear as a witness before the Grand Jury to give testimony. I was told that in keeping with the regulations of his department he would first have to obtain its consent before he could testify. This he readily agreed to do.

On the day following our conference with the agent I received a phone call from the tax division of the Department of Justice advising me that the Internal Revenue Department had called and requested that the matter be not presented to the Grand Jury for indictment until after the investigation had been fully completed.

I was puzzled at such a request, but asked when they expected to complete the investigation. I was informed that the Internal Revenue Department stated it would take thirty to sixty days more to finish it. I told the Assistant Attorney General that we, and not the Internal Revenue Department, had finally "broken" the case and that I was taking no chances—that I intended to submit the case to the Grand Jury now, and not thirty or sixty days from now, stating that I saw no legitimate reason to delay the indictments of Pendergast and O'Malley. To make my ultimatum more certain, I said, "I am going to submit these cases to the Grand Jury in the morning whether or not I have the testimony of an agent of the Internal Revenue Department."

When the next morning arrived, I was informed by Mr. Hartmann of the Intelligence Unit that he was ready to testify and before noon indictments against Pendergast and O'Malley were returned.

Whether or not the investigation was ever finally completed I cannot say, but of this I am certain, that before either the thirty or the sixty days had elapsed, Thomas J. Pendergast and Robert Emmett O'Malley were inmates of the Federal Penitentiary at Leavenworth, Kansas.

During the course of the investigation and development of the facts relative to the insurance case, the Bureau of Internal Revenue had been making additional investigation of Pendergast's other income for the years 1927 to 1937, inclusive. During this inquiry the Bureau had discovered that Pendergast, for many years, had been concealing income he had received from his various business enterprises. The method used to conceal his ownership in enterprises in which he was the owner or had a large interest, and to conceal his actual income from legitimate business in which he was engaged, was to have stock certificates issued and held in the names of other persons and the dividends thereon paid to these individuals. Carrying out this corrupt practice, the books of his companies were falsified and often showed payments of salaries to other persons, when actually the payments were made to himself. To keep such transactions hidden from the Government, he fraudulently procured these persons to file false income taxes, falsely stating under oath that they were the actual owners of the stocks and the actual recipients of salaries and dividends. Another method frequently used was to procure the officers and employees of corporations in which he had control to falsify the corporate books so as to show loans amounting sometimes to as much as $20,000 to have been made to themselves; when actually they merely issued a check to themselves, endorsed it, and cashed it, immediately paying the proceeds to Pendergast.

Investigation into his business connections disclosed that Pendergast either concealed dividends on stocks, or falsified the books to show loans or monies paid to him as being salaries paid to others. Investigation further showed that Pendergast not only owned and controlled the Ready-Mixed Concrete Co., the T. J. Pendergast Wholesale Liquor Co., and the W. A. Ross Construction Co., but that in fact he owned a large interest in, or had control of, six other prominent corporations; namely, Midwest Asphalt

Co., Midwest Paving Co., Sanitary Service Co., Glendale Sales Co., Midwest ProCote Co., and the Kansas City Concrete Pipe Co. But the investigation showed that during all these years Pendergast had never reported any income at all from any of these corporations except the Ready-Mixed Concrete Company, the T. J. Pendergast Wholesale Liquor Co., and the W. A. Ross Construction Co. It was discovered that he used another subterfuge to conceal his actual income by the scrupulous avoidance of all except the most negligible record evidence. Rarely did he use a bank account. All dividends and fictitious salaries, as well as all payment of almost every nature, he required to be made to him in currency. Even on the infrequent occasions when he accepted checks for apparently legitimate purposes they were immediately converted into currency and no records whatsoever kept. Virtually all of his expenditures over the years were made in currency. Large expenditures sent to other cities he covered by procuring others to purchase in their names drafts or telegraph money orders. Some expenditures were transmitted by express. Even when sojourning in another city and having money sent to him there from Kansas City, he went to the extremity of using an assumed name. Always he attempted to conceal. During the year 1935, the evidence disclosed that he spent in currency at least $160,509.21 above and beyond the amounts reported by him as taxable and the amounts the Government knew he borrowed. During 1936, the evidence revealed that he spent in currency at least $365,456.15 above and beyond the amounts reported by him as taxable income.

Investigation also showed that Pendergast was an inveterate bettor on horse races, and that all of his bets were made in currency, whether in Kansas City or elsewhere. As a matter of fact he was one of the biggest plungers on the American turf. In 1936 he wagered at least $74,000 on horse races. In 1935 he wagered at least $161,328.75 on horse races, and actually lost the sum of $600,000. This additional evidence not only proved that he had defrauded the Government in 1935 and 1936, but revealed that during the period of 1927 to 1937, a period of ten years, Pendergast by employing the methods heretofore outlined had consistently concealed his real income during every one of those years and had defrauded the Government of huge amounts of income taxes. It established beyond doubt that Pendergast had feloniously concealed from the Government and wilfully failed to report income during those ten years in the amount of $1,040,746.56; that he had defrauded the Government of income taxes amounting to $551,078.75.

Two of the men used by Boss Pendergast in his efforts to cover up the real income received in his business enterprises were E. L. Schneider, Secretary and Treasurer of the Ready-Mixed Concrete Company, and old Captain Elijah Matheus, who, as heretofore related, for many years acted in the capacity of chief greeter of callers and door-keeper at the boss's political sanctum in 1908 Main Street.

The records of the Ready-Mixed Concrete Company showed Captain Matheus as the owner of a sizable block of its stock. During the years 1935 and 1936, according to the dividend record accounts, the old Captain had received annual dividends of approximately $30,000 each year. The Captain had duly made income tax returns for the years and had actually reported these amounts as income received and paid the tax to the Collector of Internal Revenue.

The agents of the government being a little skeptical on the subject of ownership of this stock, interviewed the old Captain, who steadfastly maintained that he owned the stock and had received the dividends from the company. When queried as to what disposition he made of this sum of money, he merely shook his head and sadly admitted he had wasted it in riotous living. The agents, in checking up the Captain's bank accounts, discovered he was indebted to the bank in the sum of $400, evidenced by a note upon which he had made small payments at intervals during these years of plenty. When the Captain was confronted with this conflicting fact he still remained adamant, saying, "Well, I was just nigger-rich and threw my money away and just overlooked paying my note."

I realized this old gentleman was one of those rare individuals, who would remain loyal to his boss no matter what fate might befall him. I therefore asked him to come into my office for a private conference. I frankly stated that we did not believe his story and that there was the likelihood of his being indicted for perjury if he continued to maintain that he was the owner of this stock and had collected the dividends as his own income.

I informed him that I knew his motive was to protect Pendergast but that we didn't need his testimony to indict or convict Pendergast, for we had overwhelming evidence for that purpose. I then suggested that he see

Pendergast and tell him exactly the facts I had related to him and return the next day.

On the following day the Captain came to my office and said he was ready to tell the truth concerning the stock and dividends. He said, "I didn't own a share of the stock nor did I get a penny of the dividends paid me."

The last time I saw the gallant and loyal old steamboat Captain, who forsook the muddy waters of the Missouri River for the equally muddy waters of Missouri politics, was in 1942 on the circus grounds where I engaged him in a friendly chat.

Schneider was interviewed by revenue agents at intervals for a period of two weeks. He answered, the agents said, many questions pertaining to business of the Ready-Mixed Concrete Company, but when the really important questions were hurled at him, he resorted to his right to refuse an answer on the ground that the answer might tend to incriminate him. This situation stymied the agents and their efforts were almost fruitless.

It was decided that he be subjected to examination before the Grand Jury. After many hours of grilling before that body, my assistants reported that no evidence of importance was obtained from this witness; that he still maintained his constitutional right to refuse to answer.

As a last resort, it was decided by our office and the revenue agents that I should have a personal conference with him and make a final effort to break him. Accordingly, I asked him to come into my office and informed him that while he had taken care of himself in most instances relative to his testimony before the Grand Jury, in one or two respects he had left himself open to indictment for perjury. I told him we did not want to be forced to send him to the penitentiary as we realized that whatever acts he had committed in handling the records of the Ready-Mixed Company were done at the direction of Pendergast.

Finally I said, "Mr. Schneider, I am going to give you until 4 P.M. this afternoon to make up your mind whether or not you will tell the whole story." I then suggested that he advise with his lawyer and friends, and intimated that it might be well to consult with Boss Pendergast and let him also know of his present predicament.

At exactly four o'clock that afternoon, Schneider appeared at my office accompanied by a prominent attorney who advised me that Mr. Schneider was prepared to tell the story in full.

In the presence of his attorney, Mr. Schneider related to me briefly the machinations and subterfuge used in handling the books and records of the Ready-Mixed Concrete Company, and how the stock books and certificates of stock had been issued at the instigation of Pendergast to certain persons, and dividends from these stock certificates were paid to these people, but how in the end the money reached the pockets of Pendergast himself. After listening to the story I took him in for examination before the Grand Jury. Later in the afternoon I turned him over to Mr. Hartmann, the agent in charge of the investigation, who examined him in detail as to the transactions and manipulations. Before leaving the Federal Building Mr. Schneider appeared again at my office and advised me that he felt much better since he had revealed the truth of the matter. He said that he had been under a terrific strain for many weeks and he felt that his action would relieve him of this anxiety and mental worry. I requested that he return to the Federal Building the next morning as the agents wished to question him more fully. The next morning he appeared at the office apparently in good spirits and remained at the Federal Building until around eleven o'clock that day, which, as I remember, was on Friday. At that time I excused him for further service before the Grand Jury with the understanding that he would remain at the call of the revenue agents to give such information as they might desire.

On Monday before the noon hour, I received a call from a reporter who said that Schneider's car had been found on one of the bridges spanning the Missouri River; that the books and records of the Ready-Mixed Concrete Company were on the seat of the car and that notes addressed to his wife evidencing his intention to commit suicide had also been found in the car. During the next three days many wild conjectures arose. No person had seen him make the leap from the bridge to the Missouri River waters. But at the end of three days his body came to the surface.

I was very much surprised and shocked at this tragic occurrence. When I had last seen him he was in apparently good spirits and could have had no such intentions when he left the Federal Building. Immediately following this news, I called upon the Federal Bureau of Investigation to make an inquiry into the disappearance of the man and after questioning the members of his family, ascertained the fact that he became extremely nervous and jittery during the week end. On the morning of the tragedy he had advised his wife that he was going to the office of the revenue agents and would take with him the complete records of the Ready-Mixed Concrete Company for their examination. He had placed the same in the car for that purpose and was preparing to leave home, when he received a telephone call which he answered, and advised his wife that the Director of Police was coming to see him. In a short time, according to the testimony of his wife, Otto Higgins, the Director of Police, drove up to the home and briefly conferred with her husband. In a short time Mr. Schneider drove away in his car and apparently Director of Police Higgins was the last man who ever saw him alive. Higgins was later indicted and pleaded guilty to income tax evasion and served a term in the Federal Prison in Leavenworth, Kansas. What really caused Edward Schneider to seek his refuge in the muddy waters of the Missouri is still an unsolved mystery.

In spite of the loss of this key witness, the agents of the Bureau built up proof of Pendergast's business manipulations aside from the sums of money he had received from the insurance companies, wherein he had defrauded the Government of hundreds of thousands of dollars. It was clearly evident that we could sustain the indictments with reference to this additional income.

Pendergast showed up at the Federal Building less than two hours after the indictment, accompanied by his son, T. J. Pendergast, Jr., and his nephew, James M. Pendergast. His attorneys, John G. Madden and R. R. Brewster, had arrived ahead of him. The news of the indictment spread rapidly, and a flock of reporters were waiting for Pendergast. Joseph Murphy, Deputy U. S. Marshal, was getting the fingerprint materials ready. The reporters wanted to get a picture of the boss having his fingerprints recorded. "Do you want them to photograph you having your prints taken, Mr. Pendergast?" Murphy asked. "Hell, they have a million," Pendergast replied.

After he was fingerprinted, one of his attorneys attempted to assist him in putting on his overcoat. He pulled away rather brusquely and said, "I'm all right. Christ was crucified on Good Friday." It happened to be coincidental that the first indictment was returned on Good Friday. When Robert Emmett O'Malley was being sought to be notified of his indictment he was attending a church in Baltimore, Maryland.

Pendergast's followers were stunned when they learned of the indictment. City Manager McElroy and Chief of Police Higgins were glum and had little to say. The rank and file felt that their leader could clear himself. No one had ever won a fight against him when the chips were down. His lawyers could pull him out on some technicality. His friends in Jefferson City muttered, "It's too bad," and went home for their Easter vacations. Senator Truman, who had been in Kansas City for several days, was driving back to Washington when the news of his friend's indictment reached him. He was very much disturbed over the whole matter. On April 13, City Manager McElroy resigned after thirteen years of running the affairs of Kansas City along lines dictated by Boss Pendergast. He saw the handwriting on the wall. Mayor Bryce C. Smith, who had been serving as a window dressing for the Pendergast organization and playing second fiddle to

McElroy, took over the task of running the city. Newsmen got wind of the McElroy resignation a few hours in advance. They noticed that the red light and siren, those impressive marks of authority, had been removed from McElroy's car.

Things were happening fast in Kansas City. On April 12, Government agents arrested thirteen men in Kansas City on the charge of violating the narcotic laws. These dope distributors were handling $1,000,000 worth of heroin a month in the Kansas City drug traffic. Among those arrested were James "Guinea Pig" Abbott, who weighed over 450 pounds and who was called "the biggest dope peddler in the world"; Angelo Donnici, "Mayor of East Ninth Street," and others who had found "protection" in Kansas City during the era of Johnny Lazia and Boss Pendergast. "Guinea Pig" Abbott, incidentally, was a brother-in-law of Joe Lusco, who vied with Lazia for control of the Italian wing of the Pendergast machine. On April 11, Circuit Judge Allen C. Southern told the Judiciary Committee of the Missouri House that "gamblers are unlawfully taking from the pockets of the citizens of Kansas City three times the total cost of operation of the city." He estimated that the annual "take" of Kansas City gamblers approximated $20,000,000.

Coincidental with the Pendergast case in the Federal Court was the case of Charles V. Carollo, head of the Kansas City gambling syndicate, and acknowledged successor to the late Johnny Lazia. Judge Merrill E. Otis occupied the bench during the Pendergast, O'Malley and Carollo trials.

He conducted these sensational and highly-publicized

legal proceedings with all the dignity and humanity associated with the best traditions of the bench and bar.

Just before the Pendergast trial was to get under way Judge Otis and I were advised that the defendants Pendergast and O'Malley were going to enter pleas of guilty. This information was a severe blow to those who had worshiped and believed in the boss. His friends could not believe the news when they heard it. His followers were not the only ones who could not believe this to be a fact. On the morning the plea was docketed for hearing, I refused to release to the press copies of a written statement of facts I was to present to the court until I had seen the defendant enter the courtroom and heard with my own ears the plea of guilty.

By pleading guilty, Pendergast threw himself upon the mercy of the court. He also averted further Federal prosecution, as well as open court testimony on his financial rake-offs from the diverse activities of his political machine. Too many prominent persons in Kansas City would have been embarrassed had the whole sordid story of the Pendergast machine been drawn from the witness stand. The boss and his attorneys were fully aware of this. The only smart thing to do was to trust to the leniency of the court. Whatever the verdict, it could not be as humiliating as a long-drawn-out trial.

I presented my findings of fraud and tax evasion, at the request of Judge Otis, and I outlined the insurance case manipulations and the concealment of income pretty much in the factual manner that I have used in this chapter. I eschewed oratory and dramatics. There was enough drama in the packed courtroom that day. Little that I might say could add to the stark tragedy of a man at bay and caught in a mesh of his own making. Quietly sitting there between his son and his nephew, listening to the charges of the Government, and the impassioned pleas of his defense lawyers, Pendergast was a broken old man. He had come to the end of his trail.

John G. Madden, attorney for Pendergast, said to the court: "I want to allude to the statement made by counsel that this defendant, throughout the years, has indulged in betting on the racing of horses. That is true. It has been a mania with him.

"Men are not of strength without weakness. There is no man who does not have the chink in the armor that may destroy him. It was a mania with this defendant, and his losses were terrific."

R. R. Brewster, another attorney, also made an eloquent plea that clemency be shown his client. He too made quite a point of the defendant's penchant for betting on the horses. "I want to address myself, if I may, just for a moment to this question of the defendant gambling or betting upon race horses . . . I asked this defendant just yesterday what there was about this thing that had led him on to ruin. Was it the desire for gain? Was it because he thought he could win in betting upon the horses in these races far away? I wanted to know what it was that was behind it all, and I asked him how he did it. Did he plan days ahead? Did he make his bets the day before the race was run? Did he only care to see the horses down the stretch when he was present at the race?

"His answer was, 'I don't know what it is, but it has

been with me all my life since I came from St. Joseph here.' A little bit at first, gradually growing and then some ten years ago in its full tide.

"He told me that when the afternoon was here, 2:30, 3 o'clock, he would go into a little room, and there he would take the form sheet, and with the advice of a friend of his he would handicap these horses, and then he would sit with the telephone at his ear and he would hear a call, 'They're at the post.' Later, 'They're off,' and so over that telephone, by ear and not by eye, he watched those horses run to the finish line—all the thrill that can ever come to any man, for that which possesses him and which he cannot down."

SENTENCE

JUDGE MERRILL E. OTIS sentenced Pendergast to fifteen months in prison, fined him $10,000, and decreed that he was to pay back taxes, penalties, and interest to the amount of $434,000. On a second count he was sentenced to three more years, but these he was not to serve because of a probationary decree. Thus ended a case that had been months in the making, and Tom Pendergast's notorious career as boss of Kansas City came to its close. Many expected a more severe sentence. Many newspaper editors, particularly those in St. Louis, bitterly assailed the verdict. "The enormity of Pendergast's crime is such it merited a far heavier sentence," said the St. Louis *Post-Dispatch*.

Pendergast was allowed to return to his home before starting the trip to Leavenworth Penitentiary. "When

Thomas J. Pendergast left the Federal Building today in an automobile after being sentenced to imprisonment for income-tax evasion, he dropped James M. Pendergast, his nephew, at the Jackson County Democratic Club, 1908 Main Street, with the understanding that the nephew was to take over the leadership of the Pendergast political machine." [1]

Robert Emmett O'Malley, who pleaded guilty along with Pendergast, was also sentenced to serve a prison term in Leavenworth. Henry Dillingham, United States Marshal, when asked if Pendergast and O'Malley were going to prison together, replied: "They went down together. Maybe they'll go up together."

Pendergast was driven to Leavenworth Penitentiary by his son, Thomas J. Pendergast, Jr., and his nephew and political successor, James M. Pendergast. He was made to don a blue denim uniform, and spent the usual thirty days in quarantine. O'Malley arrived at the prison just an hour before the time limit allowed him. He had been born in Leavenworth, Kansas, in 1874. Now he was returning to his home town, a felon.

Otto Higgins, Chief of Police in Kansas City, was indicted in the cleanup of the Pendergast machine, and he also went to the penitentiary. John J. Pryor, of the Boyle-Pryor Construction Company, a company that had fattened on favored contracts during the lush years of the Pendergast rule, met his fate in Federal Court for income-tax evasion. Matthew Murray, a staunch Pendergast man who was the Director of the Public Works

[1] *The New York Times,* May 23, 1939. Dispatch from Kansas City was dated May 22.

Administration for the State of Missouri as well as Director of Public Works of Kansas City, was brought before the Federal Court under indictment and convicted of income-tax evasion. So one by one the key men who aided and abetted Pendergast over the years were caught in the net of the law. The State of Missouri took the control of the Kansas City police force out of the city's hands and placed it under the supervision of the State administration.

Thus fell one of the greatest political dynasties ever created in America.

LEAVENWORTH

THERE were enough Pendergast henchmen in Leavenworth Penitentiary when Pendergast arrived there to form a club, had they been allowed to hold a reunion with their boss. A great many of the vote fraud crowd were doing time there. Even in prison Pendergast was looked upon as a "big shot" calling for special treatment. He was a sick man for a greater part of the time, and he had lost the old arrogance that comes with unchallenged leadership. The spring went from his step. His prison photographs, released to the public, and thereby setting a precedent, revealed a face lined with tragedy. The publication of these pictures, a most unusual departure from established custom, was the most humiliating experience connected with his long career.

A press dispatch from Leavenworth, Kansas, dated January 6, 1940, gives us an intimate picture of his prison life. It read: "The first inmate to arise each morning in the

Leavenworth Penitentiary hospital is T. J. Pendergast. He is dressed, washed and standing in his doorway before 5 o'clock. At that hour sounds the clump of the newspaper distributor's stride down the corridor of Ward B. When the paper drops in front of the former boss's tiny room, he reaches out, takes it up and returns to his bed. He reads steadily for the next hour in the silence of the huge prison. At 6:00 (summer) or 6:15 (winter) there comes the clang of the morning bell. Throughout the prison, the voices of 3,000 men hum. In a few moments the cell doors clang open, the men march down the hallways and into the dining room. Pendergast does not. He remains in his room, his breakfast going to him on a tray. Sometimes he eats so little, the food appears untouched. At any event, he has read virtually all the paper, which reaches him as it does all prisoners, uncensored. Few men have followed the current events of the world more closely than Pendergast. He used to chide reporters for their failure to know and remember what appeared in their own papers. He has not broken that lifelong habit of careful reading. Aside from his papers (the morning and afternoon editions of *The Star*) he reads little except *Reader's Digest.*

"Save for a few days shortly after he had completed his 30 days in the observation ward following his admittance to the prison, he has been assigned to the hospital. There was a brief period when he took his place in the normal routine of the prisoners. He was placed in 'C' cellhouse on the 'flag,' the convict's term for the ground floor. That was a concession to his heart ailment and age. After a few days he suffered a dangerous heart attack, and was removed to the hospital. He has had no other setbacks, contrary to rumor, but his condition, both as a result of his heart ailment and an intestinal disorder has demanded constant residence in the hospital. There he has a bed with springs, instead of the steel slats upon which the ordinary convict reclines. He is well equipped to do the details to which he is assigned. It is his task to compile the medical case history of convict patients. When the physician is examining an inmate, he dictates his findings to Pendergast. The boss sets them down in his firm, clear, rather rotund handwriting. That afternoon or night he transfers them to a more permanent medium, the case ledger. Sometimes this work requires only 30 minutes or so, but if the hospital has had a run of examinations, he may labor over the journal several hours.

"He has no confidantes. Dr. Ludwig Muench, of St. Louis, under sentence in the famous baby hoax case, often spent hours at night gossiping with him. Muench was a brilliant aid to the hospital staff, but was transferred to Federal prison hospital, Springfield, Mo., four months ago. Now Pendergast spends his leisure with his papers, magazines, or with headphones clamped on, listening to the radio. Few men in the history of the prison have aroused the speculation among the inmates that Pendergast did when he was indicted. Bets were laid that he would never go to trial; the cynical contended he had too much power even to do time. When he pleaded guilty and was sentenced to 15 months, the prison simmered with excitement and indignation. A wave of self-pity engulfed the great body of convicts. They pointed to their own cases, and agreed that Pendergast was the perfect example of the old saw—'the bigger the crook, the lighter the punishment.'

"At the same time, a thousand tales of Kansas City's iniquities under the old regime swept through the 3,000 men. They related how cheaply you could buy a cop under the Pendergast reign, how you paid lip service to the machine, and got away with any racket if you cut the proper men in. The mood of anger had become dissipated by the time Pendergast and R. E. O'Malley, his stooge, arrived—now the convicts were filled with curiosity. Some of their rancor towards Pendergast remained, but their chief concern was to discover whether he was, in their parlance, a 'Square John.' When he suffered his heart attack and was removed to the hospital, a cry of favoritism spread through the prison. The belief that his sickness was simulated died when the hospital staff continued to keep him under observation. Finally the men lost interest in him. They turned their attention to O'Malley, Charles V. Carollo, Otto P. Higgins and others. There is no basis for the story that Pendergast amused himself by betting fabulously imaginary sums on the horses. His passion for betting was probably the largest contributing factor to his downfall. He admitted it led to his ruin. But today he refuses even to discuss the outcome of a race." [1]

I would like to pause at this point to clarify, if I can, some of the conflicting ideas concerning the personality of this political titan. In an effort to look behind the curtain and see the real human side of T. J. Pendergast, I went over the field of his personal and political intimates who might be willing to furnish me a genuine picture of

[1] Kansas City *Star*, January 7, 1940.

the man. The first man I interviewed had known the boss personally for more than forty years and during most of that time was aligned with him politically as were many other prominent Democrats in Kansas City and Jackson County. He said to me, "Pendergast had an unusual brain. If he had attended West Point in his youth, he would doubtless have become a great general."

My informant went on: "He had a wonderful memory," and with a twinkle in his eye smilingly added, "also a very convenient one if the occasion demanded." I pressed him for an illustration, and he recalled the candidacy of a prominent lawyer for a circuit judgeship in which a group of attorneys called upon Mr. Pendergast in his behalf and asked for support. The boss, he said, stated that he had picked another for the place and if this man would withdraw he would put him upon the ticket for the next vacancy on the bench. But, when the time arrived he failed to remember his promise and set up another candidate.

I asked him if sentiment seemed to be a Pendergast characteristic. He replied without a moment's hesitation that in the many years of his association with Pendergast he saw little evidence of this human trait, except as it related to his brother Jim, whose memory he idolized, and the members of his own family. He discounted the doling out of dollars to the needy and the annual Christmas feasts to the city's poor as merely good political business that paid fat dividends on election day.

This old friend seemed to be an astute observer, and in my opinion an excellent judge of men. While trying to be fair in his character analysis of Pendergast, he spoke rather feelingly when he referred to the boss's manner toward most of his loyal friends and supporters. "T.J.," he said, "felt that none was his equal and apparently viewed them as mere underlings." He recalled a conversation he had with Pendergast several years ago in which he said to the boss, "John O'Neill is one of your most devoted assistants." Pendergast replied, "Yes, he's all right. I just use him to tell the boys what I want done." John P. O'Neill for many years served the Pendergast cause as one of the more able members of the City Council.

In another conversation my informant quoted Pendergast on William T. Kemper, a prominent banker and business man: "Kemper thinks he's done a lot for me—why, I helped make him what he is." My informant also recalled a story of a victory meeting of prominent Democrats many years ago in the old Baltimore Hotel in Kansas City, held for the purpose of outlining a policy for the new Democratic administration. Pendergast was present and had little to say, but one remark and gesture was typical of the man. "One thing sure, I'll not temporize with that fellow Shannon any longer," blurted Pendergast while rising from his chair. "I'm leaving, I have a horse running today." And with that remark he strode from the room.

I interviewed a veteran lawyer who had known Pendergast intimately for more than thirty-five years and had represented clients who dealt with both the administration of Kansas City and Jackson County. He related that a number of years ago the city was preparing to let a contract for the construction of a viaduct and that he represented a construction company which was interested in obtaining this contract. He prepared the bid for his client but preliminary to presenting it to the City Council he visited his friend Pendergast at his wholesale whiskey establishment at 6th and Delaware Streets. After passing the time of day he said, "I am representing (he named the firm) which is going to bid on the construction of the viaduct." T.J. said to him, "I am sorry, but you can't have it. I am going to give that contract to (naming another) company."

This attorney was a member of the bi-partisan Commission selected to formulate the charter setting up the non-partisan form of city government. He was asked by the Commission to interview Pendergast in an effort to obtain his support for the adoption of the charter. The boss readily pledged his support, saying, "These damn reformers think they take over the city government under this new charter. I can win under it as easy as under the old one."

Another incident was related by this old friend of T.J.'s concerning charges that a conspiracy existed between two contracting firms in their bids on construction of streets in the city. One of these firms was the W. A. Ross Construction Company, and the other the Davidson Construction Company. The boss had this to say to such charges: "Don't you think these firms can construct streets as cheap as anyone else?" The attorney answered, "Yes, I think they can." Then the boss replied, "Well, then they ought to be favored." Pendergast was a silent partner of the W. A. Ross Construction Company.

A Pendergast follower told me that the boss had a man

who looked after his affairs in eastern Jackson County. At one time this man was County Treasurer. One day he walked into Tom's headquarters and said to him, "I've got to have some more patronage. I've got five thousand votes out there." T.J. stopped him abruptly, scowled and said, "How many votes did you say you had?" His henchman replied, "Five thousand." Pendergast, pointing his finger at him in one of his typical gestures, said, "That's too many votes for one man to have. By God, I'll take every one of them away from you." And he did. From that day on, his friend and follower was ostracized and his power was broken. Pendergast was jealous of any follower who got too large. If a man threatened to become a rival he destroyed him politically. On these occasions sentiment meant nothing. The oft-asserted apology that Pendergast was a boss, but that he never forsook a friend or follower or went back on his word is just so much hokum. Prominent men who know better continue to perpetuate this fiction for purely political reasons. The Pendergast here described is the real Pendergast. As far as possible I have brought an objective viewpoint to the presentation of the facts. As United States District Attorney it was my job to investigate alleged violations of the Federal Statutes, and to prosecute violators, irrespective of persons. As I have said before I did not pass sentence. I did not condemn this man. He was condemned by his own deeds, and paid the penalty imposed by society upon those who flaunt the rules society formulates for its protection and preservation.

I would say that Tom Pendergast's arrogance and love of power were most obvious just after the State elections of 1932 and 1934. It was after Harry S. Truman went to the Senate that he began to boast of his prowess as a political dictator. A good friend of mine, in whose integrity and reliability I have implicit confidence, told me Pendergast had stated to him his reason for wanting his own friend in the Senate. The boss remarked that he had found out that the United States Senate did not represent the people; that most of its membership represented merely the big business interests of the country, and that he had decided he wanted to have his own emissary there.

Another friend of Pendergast told me that the boss was a person of much native intelligence but little education. He said that Pendergast, through experience and travel, had acquired some degree of polish, most of which was gained through association with men of more education than he himself possessed, and that in the latter years of his life he was able to associate with men of prominence with ease and poise. This friend stated that Pendergast's reading was confined chiefly to newspapers and periodicals; that he read these avidly. With the average person Pendergast was inclined to be formal, reticent, and at times cold, but with his intimates he was jovial, genial, and an excellent raconteur. His anecdotes were invariably about persons he knew, their characters, quirks, strength and weaknesses.

My informant told me stories illustrative of this trait in the boss. An acquaintance greeted Pendergast with servility and verbosity, and when he had gone the boss closed his fist and held his thumb upward, remarking, "He is as thin as the skin on my thumb." Of another of his henchmen he said, "When you walk in his front door you walk into his backyard."

Although Pendergast was a two-fisted drinker in his youth, he would often lecture his friends on the evils of alcohol during the latter part of his life. On one occasion a friend pointed out to Pendergast that he was engaged in the wholesale liquor business and that he could not understand this apparent paradox. Pendergast replied, "Hell, that's business. I just tell my friends what liquor actually does to them."

Pendergast was a powerful man physically. In the prize ring he might have been another John L. Sullivan, according to his friends who had witnessed the fistic exploits of his younger days. However, I heard what I believe to be a true story of one encounter that convinced me that discretion was a part of his valor. Pendergast was engaged in a verbal altercation with one of his followers when he said, "I'll break your jaw." His victim calmly replied, reaching into his hip pocket, "Tom, if you hit me, it will be the last time you ever hit a man." Pendergast hesitated, then walked abruptly away. At Democratic National Conventions excited partisans who tried to wrest a banner from Tom Pendergast did so at their own risk. When he said, "I'll break your jaw," he usually meant it.

When Pendergast was released from prison he returned to Kansas City on probation. He was allowed to live at his mansion on Ward Parkway, but he could not leave the city, and was not allowed to engage in politics. Since he was technically still a felon, his rights of citizenship were for the time-being revoked. This was a severe blow to him. He was a lonely man. His wife had forsaken him after he went to prison. This perhaps, was his crowning sorrow. He took solitary drives through the city he had long dominated. He became seriously ill, was taken to Menorah Hospital, and there, on a simple cot, he died, 9:40 P.M., January 26, 1945.

Funeral services for Pendergast, the man who had once had an audience with the Pope, were held in the Visitation Catholic Church, in Kansas City, and he was buried in Calvary Cemetery, in the same city. He was a member of the above church, and according to Monsignor Thomas B. McDonald, was a regular contributor to the Little Sisters of the Poor, a home for the aged, and many other Catholic institutions.

"I'm extremely sorry to hear of his death," said Harry S. Truman, then Vice-President of the United States. "He was my friend, and I was his." As related elsewhere, Vice-President Truman flew to Kansas City in an Army bomber to attend the funeral of his political mentor. The boss was dead, but the machine lived and could be useful.

VI

AN EVIL HERITAGE

Inheritors of the Mantle

IN REPLY to an inquiry in 1944, whether or not the name of Harry S. Truman had appeared in the investigations conducted by my office, I said: "At no time did the finger of suspicion ever point in the direction of Senator Truman."

Sincere as I then was in declaring that no legally demonstrable link existed between Mr. Truman and the mass of corruption we had unearthed; sincere as I then was in permitting Senator Hatch of New Mexico to quote my statement in the *Congressional Record;* the events of the past three years, the headlines screaming once again of vote frauds and indictments, the attempted subversion of jurymen, the rifling of a vault in the Kansas City courthouse itself in order to steal ballots impounded as evidence, make me wonder whether I was right in issuing a clean bill of health.

In a word, my observations of boss rule in Missouri renewing and flourishing during these years under countenance from a President of the United States and his executive assistants have dictated the writing of this book. Because of what has been permitted to happen in Missouri between 1944 and 1947, neither I nor any citizen has the right to extend the benefit of a doubt. We gave Pendergastism an exciting funeral, but the corpse has made a notable recovery. And, what is worse, the books which have recently been written about the subject adopt a tone of flip cynicism which is dangerous. After all, the activities of the Pendergast machine were not quaintly amusing to the men and women who lived under its iron rule.

Biographers may strive to minimize the importance of the political alliance between Tom Pendergast and Harry S. Truman, but history is history; the will to forget a fact cannot totally obscure it. Memory is short, but not short enough to dissolve the thick walls of Leavenworth prison, or to chase the Kansas City "ghost votes" back into the cemeteries from which they arose. Pendergast might have made the pages of history without an assist from his most illustrious disciple, but no serious student of our political scene can refute the assertion that Harry S. Truman's career, without the help of Boss Pendergast, would have ended far short of the White House. No Democratic candidate in Jackson County, Missouri, ambitious for elective offices, could have won or held such offices if Pendergast had pitted his machine against him. The forty to sixty thousand "ghost" votes were sufficient to offset any honest plurality the electorate could bestow. If anyone seriously doubts this, let him examine the records (those which have not been stolen) of the vote fraud cases in Kansas City. Are these vote frauds the figment of imagination? Ask some of the men who served prison terms because of their part in them.

The Pendergast-Truman alliance is one of the most

bizarre on record. The saga of the saloon keeper who rose to wealth and power, and the farm boy who became President, is stranger than fiction. Historians, confronted with proved Pendergast corruption, may well wonder how this union was ever brought about. The two men were totally different. They sprang from different backgrounds. Even their boyhood interests were unlike—Tom was strong as an ox and went in for strenuous sports; Harry wore glasses, shunned athletic contests and played the piano a great deal. Harry read books; Tom confined his reading to newspapers and the racing forms. Yet, looking back on the careers of the two men one cannot escape the conviction that Tom had most of the genius and Harry most of the luck. Harry's father made sure of this by nailing a horseshoe over the door of his house in Lamar, Missouri, the very day Harry was born. Judging by the record of events, this emblem of good luck has remained over Harry's political door ever since.

Look at the facts. Tom Pendergast was a tough, hard-fisted boss in Kansas City with a huge income from shady as well as legitimate sources, an invincible political organization under his thumb, and a trusted gang of henchmen ready to do his bidding. Whatever the job called for, he always had a man who could do it. If Harry Truman read the newspapers he knew that the Jackson County Democratic Club was not a body of reformers working for the purity of the ballot. Yet he became a member of this club. Unless he has resigned since these lines were written he is still its vice-president in good standing. That the Jackson County Democratic Club is simply a high-sounding title for the Pendergast machine everyone knows. Harry Truman was a farmer and road overseer. Seated on a road grader behind Missouri mules, he could skin a culvert with the best of them. He hailed everyone who passed by and called them by their first names. Next to having kinfolks, this ability to remember names and faces is the most valuable political asset in county politics. The question arises why a man like Pendergast would choose an honest farmer like Truman to run for office on the Pendergast ticket. Did Harry Truman accept the label "Pendergast man" without knowing what it implied? Once a Pendergast man always a Pendergast man. That is a political axiom in Kansas City.

Knowing Truman and knowing Pendergast it is difficult to understand why they joined forces. Some are of the opinion that the boss wanted an honest façade on his political edifice in order to cover up what went on behind it. He often boasted of putting good men in office.

Harry Truman was impressed with Tom Pendergast's personality. He stood in awe of him. Tom bore marks of greatness, the marks of the born leader. His big booming voice carried authority. Truman was always modest. He quickly acknowledged his limitations. I doubt if any man ever entered the United States Senate with more humility and self-depreciation. Tom Pendergast was one of the first political "big shots" Truman had met. You could not look into that big Irish face and ever forget it. Tom had peculiar eyes. They were large, cold, cat-like and inscrutable. They nailed you with an almost hypnotic gaze. You were either his friend or his enemy. There was no compromise with an elemental force like Pendergast. Twelve years older than Truman, he caught and held the younger man's respect. Truman was pleased to be on friendly terms with a man who could make or break a candidate with the nod of his head. I am not improvising a character for the sake of a phrase. The "country-boy" complex is one the President was never ashamed of, and he often referred to himself as "just a country-boy from Missouri" in his speeches in the Senate. Veteran reporters observed this on the occasions when the then Senator Truman emerged from White House conferences with President Roosevelt, and again at Fulton, Missouri, when he sat on the same platform with Winston Churchill. Since then he has met and shaken hands with the leaders of many countries, but I doubt if any handshake ever meant more to him than the first one "Big Tom" gave him.

President Truman's biographers have made it abundantly clear that he never looked upon the boss as a corrupt politician but simply as the man who gave him his political start. His gratitude increased as he went up the ladder. "Tom never asked me to do a dishonest deed . . . He was always honest with me, and when he made a promise he kept it. If he told me something I knew it was the truth."[1] In 1937, when President Roosevelt wanted Senator Truman to vote for Alben Barkley for the Majority leadership of the Senate, Jim Farley telephoned Tom Pendergast and asked Tom to use his influence with Truman. Truman had pledged his vote to Pat Harrison. "Tom Pendergast phoned me and asked me to vote for Barkley," Truman told newsman William

[1] McNaughton and Henmeyer, *This Man Truman,* New York: Whittlesey House, 1945.

P. Helm, "and I had to turn him down. Jim Aylward phoned me, too. I didn't mind turning Jim down, not so much, anyhow, but to say 'no' to Tom was one of the hardest things I ever had to do."[1]

If we analyze these and subsequent utterances of Harry Truman they seem to say, in effect, "I'd rather be loyal to Pendergast than be President of the United States." In short, gratitude for past political favors transcends responsibility to the people of the United States. We will go on having Kansas City vote fraud scandals as long as gratitude to bosses is made the *leit motif* of full-length biographies.

The facts of Harry Truman's early days are known to all by now. I am concerned chiefly with his association with the Pendergast machine. In 1922, when Tom was looking for a candidate for the eastern judgeship of County Court in Jackson County, Missouri, his nephew Jim recommended Harry Truman. Jim had met Truman at an Army camp and had taken a liking to him. He also knew that Truman had enough friends and relatives to roll up a sizable vote. Irritated by the insurrection of Miles Bulger, Tom was quite happy to name a candidate who would work for the "Goat" faction without trying to get control of the machinery. Harry Truman's father had been a faithful worker for the "Goats" and Harry had cut his political eye teeth by ringing doorbells in the polling of precincts on election day. This gave rise to the quip that Harry had been "weaned on goat politics." When the judgeship was dangled in front

[1] William P. Helm, *Harry Truman: A Political Biography,* New York: Duell, Sloan and Pearce, 1947.

of Truman he accepted the honor and entered into the campaign with enthusiasm. He won. From that day on he became known as "Judge" Truman.

This term "Judge" needs a bit of explaining. The judges of the County Court in Jackson County were not judges in the real sense of the term. The County Court has no judicial functions but is simply a County commission, and the so-called judges are nothing more than commissioners. The County Court is an important part of the political system because it has so much patronage at its disposal and because it is in charge and control of expenditures in the building of the County's roads and highways, as well as the erection and maintenance of all buildings constructed by the County. Its patronage includes jobs from road overseers to highway engineers, from elevator operators to superintendents of County buildings and institutions. The County Court has authority over the letting of all County contracts; it fixes the tax levies for County purposes and has the management and control of all charitable institutions operated by the County. From a political standpoint the County Court was Jackson County's most powerful agency. It was to Pendergast's advantage to have friendly judges in this contract-letting body. He had concrete to sell.

Judge Truman ran again in 1924 and was defeated. Something had gone wrong. Pendergast was not accustomed to seeing his men left high and dry, so in 1926, consistent with his policy of sticking by his men, he supported Harry Truman in the race for presiding judge of the County Court. Truman won and held this important job for two terms. The *Missouri Manual,* an official State publication, is authority for the statement that Judge Truman and other members of the court handled the spending of more than $60,000,000 of the County's funds during his incumbency.

This was a period of extensive State and County road building, and an era of construction of many new public buildings in Jackson County. Kansas City's grandiose Ten Year Plan was being put through. Pendergast, as we have seen, was then engaged in one of the most prosperous enterprises in Kansas City, known as the Ready-Mixed Concrete Company, wherein the concrete was mixed at the plant and delivered by trucks to the place of construction. In this business he exercised what amounted to a monopoly. His product was sold direct to the contractors engaged in the building project. Whenever the contract provided for the use of concrete in construction Pendergast's concern was most likely to receive an order to furnish it. Smaller concerns engaged in this enterprise became unable to compete with the Ready-Mixed Concrete Company operated by the boss himself. Contractors literally had to use the Pendergast product or else. If a Pendergast competitor tried to muscle in, it was customary for an inspector to chip off a piece of the concrete, examine it and then report to the contractor that the material did not meet specifications. The hint was dropped that if Ready-Mixed was used everything would be acceptable.

Pendergast did not confine his business to concrete in this era of progress. As we know, he was a full partner in the W. A. Ross Construction Company which engaged in both street and highway building, and the investigation carried on by our office and the Treasury Department disclosed that T. J. Pendergast was owner of the controlling interest in five other corporations engaged in the manufacture or sale of materials used in building and other construction, and that such products were almost universally used in construction in Kansas City and Jackson County during the late years of the Pendergast regime. Mr. Truman defended this by saying that the Pendergast products were as good as any other and just as cheap.

Yet when Truman was Senator and was organizing his committee to investigate the letting of war contracts he said in a speech: "Our records will show that more than three billion dollars in defense contracts have been let to just four companies. I am not opposed to that if it is absolutely necessary, but there is not any reason why those four companies could not make a distribution of the three billion dollars of contracts in such a way that the little people would not be put out of business by priorities and things of that kind which are now staring them in the face."

When the year 1934 rolled around Judge Truman, as he was then, began looking ahead. The County Collector's job was the richest plum in the Pendergast basket. This office paid anywhere from $25,000 to $30,000 in fees annually. Judge Truman coveted this job above all others, for it would provide a competency for himself and his family in the years to come. Pendergast, in his characteristic manner, rebuffed him and told him that he had promised the job to another man, and that was that. It looked for a while as if the Truman luck was running out.

On March 27, 1934, the Pendergast machine became involved in the bloody and shocking election outrages which I have described in a previous chapter. The sensibilities of all decent people in Kansas City were offended, and enraged people in other parts of Missouri raised their voices in protest. In all his years of power Pendergast had never had to face such a barrage of angry criticism. The breakdown of law and order in Kansas City had given Missouri an evil name. Missourians are an easy-going people, but don't push them too far. They are fiercely proud of their State and they resent slurs from the outside. Having the details of the bloody election of 1934 spread across the front pages of the nation's newspapers made Missourians good and mad. They turned their wrath on Pendergast and his crowd. Even small town newspaper editors thought it their duty to write vitriolic editorials about the mess in Kansas City. The boss was still entrenched throughout the State and had faithful followers in every County courthouse, but this wave of indignation was so strong and threatening that the prospects of a Pendergast victory in the State primary election were anything but bright.

The most important office involved in that election was that of United States Senator. Pendergast had recognized the importance of having one of his followers in Washington. The first public announcement of Pendergast on the subject heralded the possible entrance into the race of our old acquaintance Congressman Joseph B.

Shannon, formerly the arch foe but now the ally of Pendergast. Mr. Shannon made a hurried trip from Washington to Missouri and began a canvass of the situation over the State. What he discovered did not please him. It did not take this foxy old political strategist very long to see that the Democrats of St. Louis and outstate counties would look with disfavor upon any candidate backed by the machine that had brought such shame upon Missouri's fair name. Shannon smilingly thanked his friend Pendergast, but firmly declined the honor. He liked, he said, his job in the House of Representatives.

Boss Pendergast continued his search for a candidate. James Aylward, who as County Chairman, exhorted the political faithful on the eve of every election, and who had recently been elevated to membership on the Democratic National Committee, was next tendered this place on the Pendergast slate, but the wily Jim, who had received his political training at the knee of his old friend Joe Shannon, contemplated the "honor" with profound pleasure but had such misgivings over the outcome that he, too, "reluctantly" declined.

Pendergast called in the boys for another huddle. Other names were discussed. It has been authoritatively stated that Jim Aylward suggested the name of Judge Harry Truman. The boss toyed with the idea for only a moment and then instructed his nephew Jim and Aylward to get in touch with Truman, who was absent from the city, and advise him of his selection. The two men arranged to meet the prospective candidate in Sedalia, Missouri. The meeting was held and the two emissaries of the boss broke the news to Judge Truman that he was to be the machine's candidate for United States Senator. Truman, therefore, was Pendergast's third choice for the job.

Back in Washington, Joe Shannon looked upon Pendergast's choice of Truman with some misgivings. He confided his opinion to newsman Bill Helm. "I never heard of him," Helm remarked. "That's the trouble, Brother Helm. Hardly anybody outside of Jackson County knows him or of him. He's practically unknown, and that isn't going to help the ticket. . . . I don't think he is heavy enough for the Senate. I can't imagine him there and I doubt if he can be elected." For once Joe Shannon underestimated Pendergast's political genius. The boss still had a few tricks up his sleeve.

Since I had a personal interest in the 1934 senatorial race, I know that I run the risk of being accused of bringing up issues for the sake of evening an old score. But, since I am concerned with a page of actual history, I must record that the candidate Tom Pendergast wanted Truman to run against in 1934 was my brother, Congressman J. L. Milligan, who had served the people of the Third Missouri District faithfully and well for thirteen years.

After the Truman announcement, a third candidate entered the field, another veteran member of Congress, John Cochran of St. Louis. Cochran was assured of a huge segment of Democratic votes in and around St. Louis, and this, his followers reasoned, would be enough to offset the usual block of Pendergast votes in Kansas City and Jackson County. Old Tom was delighted with this three-cornered fight in the primary election. It meant a split in the votes, and this would work to the advantage of his candidate. And so it turned out. Judge Truman received in Kansas City and Jackson County a total of 138,423 votes, while his opponents' combined vote was only 10,437 (according to the election returns). Truman won the statewide nomination by a plurality of 41,000 votes. Please bear in mind that at this time Pendergast had at his disposal from forty to sixty thousand "ghost" votes.

Since 1934 was a Roosevelt year, Harry Truman went on to victory over a Republican candidate in the November election and took his seat in the United States Senate. By the time his first term ended a great many things had happened. Among other things a thorough and searching investigation of the 1936 general election in Kansas City had resulted in the indictment and conviction of 259 citizens for vote frauds.

The vote fraud trial implications were not lost upon Governor Lloyd C. Stark of Missouri. Following hard upon the heels of the announcement that approximately 60,000 "ghost" names were on the registration books in Kansas City and that these "ghosts" had voted in the last election, the Governor replaced the election board with entirely new commissioners, much to the chagrin of Pendergast, who had wholeheartedly supported Stark for the governorship. This unfriendly act upon the part of Stark resulted in a break between Pendergast and himself, and the break never healed. The showdown came when an appointee of the Governor on the Supreme Court came up for election. The boss let it be known that he would put a candidate in the field against him, and the fight was on, with Pendergast issuing his now famous political challenge, "Let the river take its course." This was Tom's first major political mistake. The issue was clearly drawn. Was a corrupt boss going to be allowed to pack the Missouri Supreme Court? St. Louis and outstate sections rallied to the Governor's cause and administered a stinging defeat to Pendergast. Stark, made bold by the mandate of the people, ordered the new election board to purge the registration books of Kansas City. This edict struck from the records the padded names of voters who did not exist, and for the first time in many years honest elections became a possibility in Kansas City.

In 1939 Pendergast himself was brought before the bar of justice and sentenced to prison for defrauding the Government in income taxes. His life-long friend, Robert Emmett O'Malley, former State Commissioner of Insurance, was also sent to Leavenworth Penitentiary. Another Pendergast henchman, Otto P. Higgins, former Director of the Kansas City Police Department, likewise fell victim to Federal justice. When the then Senator Truman visited his old friends in the Jackson County Democratic Club on his periodic trips home he encountered an increasing number of long faces. Things were not going so well at 1908 Main Street. As we have seen the Government's broom was making a clean sweep. John Pryor, favored contractor of the machine, paid his debt to society along with Matthew Murray, who occupied the dual role of City Engineer and State Director of the W.P.A. He served two years in prison. Charles Carrollo, who had become czar of the underworld following the demise of John Lazia, served long term sentences in the Federal penitentiaries at Leavenworth and Alcatraz. Lesser lights followed the same trail.

Shortly after the indictment of Pendergast I happened to be in Washington attending the annual conference of United States District Attorneys, and while there I called upon President Roosevelt. After complimenting our office on its recent work the President said, "I told Harry Truman the other day that he had better get away from that crowd out there." I, of course, knew to which "crowd" the President was referring.

My reappointment almost caused a break between President Roosevelt and Senator Truman. Truman raised his voice against me in a bitter speech delivered on the floor of the Senate the day the vote on my confirmation came up. In the same speech he attacked the Federal Judges in Kansas City who had brought Pendergast within the reach of the law. I ignored the contents of that speech. A Republican Senator whom I had never met came to my defense on that occasion and bluntly asked the Senator from Missouri if he wished to go on record as condoning vote frauds.

When the year 1940 rolled around, the political scene in Kansas City had changed beyond recognition. The Pendergast machine had been temporarily smashed, the registration books had been purged of fictitious names, and Harry Truman's closest friends were dubious about his chances of being reelected. Truman shared this belief himself. The opinion most widely held at that time was that Senator Truman would decline to run and that President Roosevelt would reward him with some appointive office. That was the understanding I had when some of my friends proposed that I enter the Democratic senatorial primary race myself. When some of Truman's own friends asked me to run, I took that as positive assurance of the then Senator's desire to stay out of the race. How could a Pendergast man get anywhere without a Pendergast?

I was also told that Senator Truman's political stock was so low that he had fears of being unable to finance his primary campaign. This was recently confirmed in William P. Helm's biography of the President. According to this same account, Senator Truman's secretary, Victor Messall, was about the only one who showed any enthusiasm over Truman's prospects. Messall went to Kansas City and lined up Jim Pendergast, successor to Tom, who heartened Truman by saying that he would vote for him if no one else did.

After Governor Lloyd Stark and I had each filed for the Senatorial nomination, the people of Missouri were all set for a discussion of state and national issues, but when Harry Truman entered the race the one issue that overshadowed all others was bossism. It became another battle between the friends and foes of Pendergast. Truman's campaign, bolstered by funds from A. F. Whitney and his Brotherhood of Railway Trainmen, gathered momentum and the summer air in Missouri was filled with the charges and countercharges of three candidates instead of two. This was the one thing I had hoped to avoid. When the votes were counted Truman was the winner in a real squeaker. He won by a plurality of 7,000 votes. The margin of victory in that heated campaign was the block of votes rounded up in St. Louis by a young man by the name of Bob Hannegan. Four years later this same Bob Hannegan was to engineer the nomination of Truman for Vice-President of the United States. Governor Stark and I both forgot in the heat of the campaign that Harry Truman had a magic force working for him—that horseshoe over the door in Lamar, Missouri. This will become more obvious when I state that at the opening of Truman's 1940 campaign Bob Hannegan was working for a St. Louis machine pledged to Governor Stark! The famous Hannegan switch meant the difference.

Preceding my announcement as a candidate for the Senate I was compelled, under the provisions of the Hatch Act, to resign my job as U. S. District Attorney, although my term had two more years to run. I had no intention of ever assuming that office again. But in September, 1940, after the primary, I received a telegram from the Department of Justice asking if I would accept reappointment as District Attorney, and I was advised that neither Senator Clark nor Senator Truman would oppose the appointment, and that Senator Hatch, author of the Hatch Act, would register no objection thereto in view of my record in that office. With these assurances I accepted the reappointment. I was duly confirmed and was soon back in the harness.

On October 1, 1940, Attorney General Jackson called me by phone and said that he and President Roosevelt had conferred concerning the advisability of starting a nationwide investigation of contributions and expenditures of national campaign funds relative to the coming November election. He further advised me that before a decision was made in the matter they wished to know whether I would come to Washington and take charge of the investigation. I readily agreed to assume this task if they so desired. I was later advised by the Attorney General of the final decision in the matter, and I was soon in Washington with a grand jury at my disposal. For a period of more than six months the investigation proceeded along the lines proposed. At the conclusion of the investigation I made a report of our findings to the Department of Justice and returned to my duties as U.S. District Attorney in Missouri.

Meanwhile in the 1940 general election Senator Truman had been reelected to the Senate over his Republican opponent by slightly over 44,000 votes, while other Democratic candidates on the National and State tickets, with one exception, received majorities ranging from 90,000 to 100,000.

However, the Democratic candidate for Governor of Missouri, sponsored by Robert Hannegan of St. Louis and the Pendergast machine of Kansas City, lost to the Republican candidate by the narrow margin of 5,000 votes according to the election returns. This defeat was a severe blow to the Democratic party and especially did it upset the Pendergast-Hannegan plans for more power and patronage.

Following the announcement of the election returns, a group of Democratic politicians met secretly in a suite of a St. Louis hotel and pondered the catastrophe that had befallen them. Ways and means were discussed to rescue the Governorship from the victorious Republican candidate. Bob Hannegan and the Pendergast forces were the prime movers in the conference.

Under the Missouri Constitution, the Speaker of the House of Representatives was under a duty to open election returns in the presence of a majority of the members of the Legislature and to publish and declare publicly the candidate for Governor having the highest number of votes. The duty of the Speaker in this regard was plain and unconditional. As a result of this clandestine conference however, the Democratic State Committee filed with the State Legislature, which happened to be overwhelmingly Democratic, a petition charging fraud and irregularities in the election, with a prayer that the Speaker be restrained from opening the returns and publishing the results. This the Legislature did by joint resolution.

The press of Missouri immediately branded this as a deliberate conspiracy to "steal the Governorship." Public indignation was aroused and the movement was denounced vehemently by honest Democrats and Republicans alike. The real scheme was to have the Democratic Legislature declare the Democratic candidate elected, but the Republican candidate filed a proceeding in the Supreme Court to obtain a writ of mandamus directing the Speaker of the House to perform his constitutional duty. The writ was unanimously granted by the Court.

The scheme of the Hannegan-Pendergast forces backfired to the discredit of all those concerned. All that was left to be done in an effort to "save face" was the institution of a contest in the Court asking for a recount of all ballots cast in the election. This proceeding soon petered out as the Republican lead increased. Thus ended an effort that made the Pendergast machine even more obnoxious to the citizens of Missouri and left Bob Hannegan a discredited leader in Missouri politics. The city of St. Louis, Democratic for many years, elected a Republican mayor by an overwhelming majority and in the State election held in November, 1942, the Democratic ticket was defeated.

Bob Hannegan, in spite of appearances, was not through politically. His friend, Senator Harry Truman, came to his rescue and had him appointed, in the face of terrific opposition, U. S. Collector of Internal Revenue for the Eastern District of Missouri. Bob had hardly become acquainted with the duties of his office before a vacancy occurred in the position of Commissioner of Internal Revenue in Washington, D. C., and through Truman's influence he was elevated to that important Federal post. The political ladder seemed to be ready for Hannegan's climb. By the time 1944 had rolled around Jim Farley had resigned as Chairman of the Democratic National Committee and then as Postmaster General, and Truman's friend Bob Hannegan took over both jobs.

The position of Chairman of the Democratic National Committee placed Hannegan in a most strategic position. As such, he became campaign manager and political adviser of President Roosevelt, who had announced his candidacy for a fourth term. He had the chance to bring his influence to bear upon the President in the choice of a running mate in the 1944 national campaign. Watching developments from the sidelines, I was almost dumbfounded at the sequence of events. Knowing what had transpired in Missouri, I could not understand President Roosevelt's selection of a discredited local boss and elevation of him to such places of power and influence. Reading stories of the President's ill health and observing pictures of him at conferences with Stalin and Churchill, I became more and more concerned about the situation. It is well known today that Roosevelt was a sick man in 1944. He was tired with years of war making and in no sense was he the old Roosevelt, the "Master Politician" of other years.

Then on a warm day in July, 1944, news flashed over the air waves that Harry S. Truman had been nominated as candidate for Vice-President of the United States at the Democratic National Convention in Chicago. Known as the "Second Missouri Compromise," this coup was brought about by Robert Hannegan, Chairman of the Democratic National Committee, who had learned his politics in the old 21st Ward in St. Louis.

Missourians were flabbergasted when they heard the exciting news. Some were fearful of the consequences, for reports of President Roosevelt's declining health raised the possibility of his death, and in that event Harry Truman would move into the White House. A lot of Missourians just couldn't see Harry Truman in F.D.R's shoes. Others were proud to know that a native Missourian had been chosen as Roosevelt's running mate.

In the early days of the campaign a man called at my office and advised me that he was gathering material for a story to be written about the then Senator Truman. He made inquiry of me as to whether or not the Senator's name figured in the investigations carried on by my office throughout the years. In this regard I replied as I have stated previously, "that in the series of investigations into vote frauds and other corruption in Kansas City, at no time did the finger of suspicion ever point in the direction of Senator Truman."

Shortly thereafter, Senator Carl Hatch of New Mexico wrote me, saying that he had been informed of my statement relative to Truman, and would I be so kind as to send him a copy of it for publication in the *Congressional Record.* I complied with the request, and it was duly printed in that publication. I have in my files a memo written in the handwriting of Harry Truman. It reads: "Maurice—Thanks a million for this—Harry." Attached thereto is a copy of the *Congressional Record* bearing my statement.

Yet less than a month after the successful election I learned through the press that Vice-President Truman had expressed himself as being opposed to my reappointment as District Attorney. I was not surprised. Neither was I especially disappointed.

I looked forward to a much needed rest. I had given some of the best years of my life to the fight against corruption in Kansas City, and the labors of any crusade against the organized underworld are not relaxing by any means. I had no further political ambitions.

Had not a series of events made the writing of this book a virtual necessity, I might have enjoyed my new-found peace of mind. When you have put your best into a fight against a corrupt machine like Tom Pendergast's, you cannot fold your hands and sit idly by when you see the blatant beast raising its head again.

This book is my small contribution to the new fight. I realize that some of my readers will feel that I am working off a grudge because I was defeated at the polls by Harry Truman. I can only assure them that this is not so, and state simply one of my deepest convictions: when you corrupt my neighbor's ballot you corrupt mine. When you destroy the right of free men to cast an honest vote you strike at the heart of democracy. If I have something to say which may serve to put the public on notice about such vicious perversions of the ballot as are the usual practice of corrupt political machines, then to remain silent would be cowardly. If I have anything to say about the cause and cure of Pendergastism, and God knows I came to grips with it at close hand, then I must invoke the privilege of free speech to make my contribution, no matter how small, to the preservation of our constitutional rights. Tom Pendergast owned Kansas City, a municipality of a half million souls, and bragged about it. He controlled practically everything in town except the Federal Building and he tried to get his hands on that. Neo-Pendergastism is not one whit less ambitious. Today, it is more menacing than ever because it has, at least, the goodwill of the President of the United States.

Shortly after Senator Truman rode to victory on the Roosevelt bandwagon in 1944 his political mentor passed away. When the new Vice-President flew to Kansas City in an Army bomber to pay his last respects to Tom Pendergast there was a good deal of eye-brow lifting and some editorial criticism, but there were many who applauded this demonstration of gratitude. It was hoped that this gesture would be the final one, that the grave would close over an alliance of more than twenty-five years. Those who indulged this hope were due for a rude awakening.

Vice-President Truman simply transferred his devotion and allegiance to James M. Pendergast, a nephew of the boss and heir to the Pendergast political dynasty. There was nothing secret about this continued affiliation with the machine. It was a tacit acceptance of the theory of boss rule.

On April 12, 1945, in the little white cottage at Warm Springs, Franklin D. Roosevelt complained of a terrific headache and slumped over dead. The shock of that tragedy fell upon the world in the dark hour just before the dawn, for the war was being fought towards a conclusion. It was a critical moment for the quiet little man from Missouri as he stood, Bible in hand, in that drama-packed room in the White House and assumed the greatest responsibility ever thrust upon an American citizen. Beset with humility and misgivings Harry Truman, with all the simplicity and sincerity in the world, implored the guidance of the Divine Power, for on that solemn occasion Harry Truman was alone and afraid.

In the weeks that immediately followed, all of us were pulling for Truman. On his shoulders was the burden of the world. It is difficult to imagine two men more unlike than Franklin D. Roosevelt and Harry S. Truman, look at them from any angle you choose. President Truman met the challenge manfully and many of his first acts were instinctively sound and salutary. His decisions were popular with the people. Then came a period characterized as "government by crony," in which the President surrounded himself with appointees from Missouri and other Middlewestern States, and with old friends of World War I days. There was nothing wrong with this, as long as he picked good men, and some of his choices were excellent; but when Jim Pendergast showed up frequently at the White House as a week-end guest and flew with the President on the "Sacred Cow," an old battered machine in Kansas City began to perk up. The Jackson County Democratic Club began to dust off the furniture and hang up new pictures.

Late in 1945 President Truman wrote and caused to be widely publicized a letter addressed to James M. Pendergast, transmitting a check in payment of his dues as a member of the Jackson County Democratic Club, at 1908 Main Street, Kansas City. The letter, written on White House stationery and bearing the date December 7, 1945, read as follows:

> "Dear Jim: I am enclosing you check for Six ($6.00) Dollars in payment of my Jackson Democratic Club dues. I hope the outfit is still going good. Sincerely Yours, Harry."

That letter and check are now framed and hang on the wall of Jim Pendergast's office. On the same wall in Jim Pendergast's office hangs a White House portrait of President Truman inscribed by the President in these words:

"To James M. Pendergast—friend, comrade and adviser."

We have devoted a good deal of space in this book to Tom Pendergast, but very little to nephew Jim, who now becomes our chief concern. James M. Pendergast was born in Kansas City fifty-four years ago, the son of Michael Pendergast, a ward politician. Michael, like his brother Tom, was born in St. Joseph, Missouri. He came to Kansas City in 1886. He was an *opera-bouffe* sort of politician and even brother Tom did not take him too seriously. He held sway in the old Tenth Ward and was City Clerk for several years. His greatest pleasure was in fighting Joe Shannon's "Rabbits." He died at the age of 62, leaving a family of six children, five of them boys. One of Mike's boys, the sober-faced Jim, soon wore a political *toga virilis* placed upon him by Uncle Tom, the "Emperor" himself. Tom let it be known that he was grooming his nephew as his successor. The heir-apparent was a devoted, plodding pupil, but not a brilliant one. If he had any world-shaking wiles and stratagems he kept them carefully masked behind a lugubrious dead-pan that was seldom cracked by a smile. He lacked his uncle's dynamic personality. But Tom strove with him diligently and gave him more and more duties to perform. When Tom went to prison he handed Jim the key to 1908 Main Street. That was a solemn and symbolical act.

Jim Pendergast takes life and politics very seriously. His home life is surrounded with the same privacy Boss Tom insisted upon. He is looked upon as a family man, and his desire to keep his private life entirely separate from his political life is to his credit. He goes in for no fanfare, and when he shows up for a conference with

President Truman in the Muehlebach Hotel in Kansas City it is not to the accompaniment of motorcycle sirens.

Jim Pendergast is heavy-set, something under six feet in height, has deep blue eyes, brown hair that is thinning rapidly, and his face, though heavy, is strong and masculine. His friends find him modest and sympathetic, tight-lipped and cautious. He prefers to work quietly behind the "iron curtain" of 1908 Main Street. His intimacy with President Truman is the crowning glory of his career, and he is not a "Johnny-Come-Lately" in the President's inner circle; for the reader will recall that it was Jim Pendergast who first brought Truman to the notice of Uncle Tom, back in 1922 when Truman was an unknown.

From the time Jim Pendergast entered Irving Grade School, and Manual High School, until he finished his legal education in the Kansas City School of Law, he was moving towards a pre-arranged goal, a goal set by his uncle, Tom Pendergast. Since the early 1890's Kansas City has been dominated by two forces: William Rockhill Nelson's Kansas City *Star*, and the Pendergast political machine. Both forces claimed credit for putting Kansas City on the map. Sometimes the two forces collided; at other times they observed a truce. Neither would countenance a serious rival. Pendergast figured that if he could control the ballot he could run Kansas City just about as he pleased, and that is just what he did. He became so puffed up with this power that he started thinking in terms of a dynasty. He looked about for a successor, and his eye fell on his nephew Jim. It looked like a very poor choice at the time. The strange pranks of fate which catapulted Harry Truman to the heights are beginning to make Tom's choice look good.

Jim Pendergast did more than just receive callers at 1908 Main Street. He and Jim Aylward took an active part in all campaigns involving Pendergast candidates. During the vote fraud investigations following the 1936 election Jim Pendergast represented his uncle in providing bonds and lawyers for the defendants. When Tom Pendergast was brought before the bar of justice Jim was always present to lend solace to the old man in his evil hour.

On that May day in 1939 when the heavy iron doors of the Federal prison closed upon Boss Pendergast, the political activities of the once most powerful figure in the arena of American politics were ended. Under the provisions of the court he was forbidden to discuss or take any part whatsoever in politics for a period of five years beginning at the conclusion of his penal servitude. He was prohibited even from discussing the subject of politics and precluded from visiting his old headquarters at 1908 Main Street. Banished from politics by the edict of the Federal judge who sentenced him, the future of his dynasty rested solely with his nephew Jim.

In the early part of 1940, the time arrived for the election of a Mayor and City Council in Kansas City. The registration lists of voters had been thoroughly purged —some fifty thousand ghost names had been stricken off by the new election board. The State Legislature had enacted legislation which removed the control and domination of the police department from the city administration and placed it in the hands of a Commission appointed by the Governor of Missouri.

The Pendergast machine was confronted with a real battle.

Many old line Democrats, who had gone along with Pendergast or had tolerated conditions under the regime, joined independent members of the party and a formidable organization was brought about by an alliance with Republicans. A non-partisan ticket was nominated and the battle was on!

James A. Reed, Democratic warrior who had so ably served Missouri in the United States Senate for eighteen years, came out of his retirement, joined with the reform forces, and gave freely of time and money in the battle against the Pendergast machine which had supported him in the years gone by. His wife, the former Nell Donnelly of industrial fame, took the leading part in the organization of women's clubs which became a definite factor in the campaign. The women of Kansas City made a determined drive, adopting as their emblem of battle "the housewife's broom." They rang doorbells, polled precincts and spread the gospel of good government in every political ward of the city.

When votes were finally counted, it was shown that the machine, for the first time in almost fifteen years, had suffered defeat. The same thing happened in 1942's city election when the city administration was elected for a term of four years due to a change in the charter.

But the Pendergast forces, in spite of the blows received in court and elections, were still able to carry on. Allied as they were with the Shannon faction, they were able to hold the line in the struggle for County offices and patronage. The Pendergast-Shannon factions were solidly entrenched in all powerful County offices and on election day this monopoly provided votes aplenty. In addition, Senator Truman had placed a close friend in the office of United States Marshal and his recommendation had been followed in the appointment of a Judge for a newly-created Federal District.

When the Senator became Vice-President in 1944, the political stock of the renascent Pendergast machine boomed, but it was nothing compared with the golden opportunities that came on Mr. Truman's succession to the Presidency. New offices, vacancies and resignations which were within the gift of the President, all kinds of Federal patronage found grateful acceptance in the ranks of good machine men, all friends of the President. Among other offices filled was that of United States District Attorney for the Western District of Missouri. It was almost like old times.

"BUY YOURSELF SOME BEER"

IF THE renewed machine had been profiting by reason of the new President's favor and grateful recollections, the time was at hand when favors were to be reciprocated.

In May, 1946, Roger Slaughter, Congressman from the 5th Congressional District of Kansas City, announced his candidacy for a third term. Slaughter had enjoyed the support of the Pendergast organization in his previous races but had incurred the displeasure of President Truman as a member of the House Rules Committee. In

July, 1946, Truman summoned Jim Pendergast to Washington and personally demanded that the Pendergast organization defeat Slaughter in the Democratic primary. On his return to Kansas City Jim Pendergast announced to the press his opposition to Slaughter.

On July 18, President Truman told a press conference in Washington that he had requested Pendergast to oppose Congressman Slaughter, and assigned as his reason the opposition of Slaughter to some of the legislation he wanted Congress to enact. He said that Slaughter had opposed "everything that I have proposed." This statement was possibly a slight exaggeration of the facts. It is well known, however, that Congressman Slaughter was opposed to the passage of the Fair Employment Practices Act, and by his vote as a member of the Rules Committee prevented this Bill from being reported to the House for consideration at the Seventy-ninth Session of Congress. He then added: "If Mr. Slaughter is right, then I am wrong." He let it be known that he would like to see his friend and neighbor Enos Axtell nominated instead of Slaughter. It might be mentioned as an amusing sidelight that the President, when asked to supply the press with Axtell's first name, had to turn to a Kansas City reporter for the information. As a matter of fact Axtell was a newcomer to Kansas City politics and virtually unknown to the voters as compared to Slaughter. Slaughter sentiment was strong before the Truman blast, and it was doubly strong after the announcement that the President was injecting himself into a purely local campaign. The word "purge" does not sit well with the American voters. It smacks too much of an ideology foreign to our way of life.

The Slaughter adherents confidently expected the President's meddling would prove to be a boomerang, but the Pendergast organization was all smiles. The President had given it a much needed "shot in the arm" by virtue of the wide publicity growing out of the incident. The machine was news again, front page news.

Congressman Slaughter, though born in an adjoining county, had lived most of his life in Jackson County and attended high school in Independence, Missouri, President Truman's home town. Later the Congressman, who boasted of Confederate ancestry, was graduated from Princeton University with an A.B. degree and then studied law in a law office in Kansas City. Following his admission to the Bar, he served for a short period as Assistant Prosecuting Attorney of Jackson County and later became a member of the Board of Education.

In 1942, while still in his late thirties, he was nominated and elected to Congress from the 5th Congressional District and re-elected in 1944. Slaughter became a member of the powerful Rules Committee during his second term and remained a member until his services in Congress ended. It has been stated upon good authority that Speaker Rayburn of the House of Representatives appointed Slaughter to the Committee at the request and insistence of Senator Truman.

Enos Axtell, a man in his early thirties, had only recently returned from service in World War II, prior to the primary election in 1946. Born in eastern Jackson County, he had studied law and he, as Slaughter had done, served for a short time as Assistant Prosecuting Attorney for Jackson County. Politically, Axtell was an unknown, without organization support of any kind, yet he decided to file as a candidate against Slaughter for the Congressional nomination in the 5th District.

Jerome Walsh, son of Frank P. Walsh prominently known for years throughout the country in labor circles, also filed with the backing of the CIO labor group. Walsh had been a candidate against Slaughter for the Democratic nomination in 1944 and was defeated by him by less than twelve hundred votes.

The 1946 primary campaign opened with these three contenders: Slaughter with the organized forces of Pendergast and Shannon factions behind his candidacy; Walsh with a labor group supporting him; while Axtell was standing alone with only his appeal as an ex-service man with a good record, and one who had returned from a victorious war.

To the political observers the race was definitely between Slaughter and Walsh, with the odds favorable to the former. Axtell, it was agreed by all, did not have a chance for the nomination.

Preceding primary day the campaign forces of Slaughter appeared before the Pendergast-dominated County Committee and requested that they be allowed challengers and watchers at the polling places and that the committee issue credentials for them. Their request was politely but firmly refused. There had been no charges of irregularities in elections held in Kansas City and Jackson County during the years following the wholesale prosecution and convictions of vote frauds, resulting from the 1936 November election. During this interlude, the Pendergast machine had had no representation on the bi-partisan election board; but in 1945 two followers had been made members of the new Board. One of these members had been closely allied with the Pendergast machine for many years and during the Federal prosecution of election frauds had acted as chief counsel for many of the defendants involved.

Not content with a statement of opposition to Slaughter, President Truman made a special trip to Jackson County on primary day to throw the weight of a personal appearance into the campaign to unseat a man he did not like. When the hubbub of a Presidential visit was over and the votes were in, the voters of Kansas City got the surprise of their lives. The unknown Axtell had won by a majority of 2300 votes. Robert Hannegan quickly informed the press that this was a vote of confidence in President Truman. Was it? Let's look at the facts.

Axtell failed to carry his own township. He lost in every ward until he came to the four key wards under control of the reborn Pendergast machine. In those wards he received 12,104 votes; Slaughter got 2072. Jim Pendergast had delivered the votes as promised. To the political observers on the Kansas City *Star* it was obvious that the new boss had delivered more than he had promised, for the glorious victory in some precincts smelled to high Heaven of fraud. The vote was far too one-sided to be accurate. In two precincts Slaughter did not receive a single vote, yet in an investigation that followed, and which we shall describe, the *Star* collected affidavits in those very precincts from voters who stated on oath that they had cast their votes for Slaughter.

When President Truman ordered Jim Pendergast to

throw the weight of the machine into the fight against Roger Slaughter he put the local machine back into the headlines. He breathed new life into an organization that for all practical purposes was as dead as a doornail. The old serpent of political corruption was not dead. It raised its ugly head again. In Missouri we have a superstition that a snake does not die until after sundown, and that it continues to move its tail hours after its head has been cut off. The President by a neat trick of political surgery had put the head and the tail of the snake together again.

An investigation of some kind seemed in order. Roy Roberts of the Kansas City *Star* instructed two returned war veterans to start checking some of the election results. They were joined by other investigators. Even the President of Kansas City University took a hand in the matter. This was a lay investigation with no official power, mind you, but it was a spontaneous movement on the part of Kansas City's long-suffering citizens to keep a vigilant eye on the doings of the renascent Pendergast crowd. The *Star* began its investigation on August 8. By September 24 it had sufficient evidence to warrant a complaint to the U.S. District Attorney, Sam M. Wear.

In brief summary this was what the *Star* had found out about the precious election: Some 45 per cent of the regularly commissioned judges and clerks at the polls for various reasons did not serve in the primary. In a scramble to make hasty substitutions, the Election Board in some instances took lists of names from ward leaders. Not only were the officials of the election suspect, but there was obvious and deliberate miscounting of ballots. In some precincts a hasty shuffle of all Democratic ballots was made. It was given out that a large number were "straight" Pendergast tickets, that is, each Pendergast candidate was credited with the number of ballots in the stack. Then a few others were tallied as voted, so there would not be the same total for each candidate. Nor was this enough. Election judges were good enough to mark ballots for voters without any indication from the voter as to which candidate he wished to support. As you can imagine, there were many and subtle variations in this corrupt practice. Among other examples of sleight-of-hand it is enough to cite the following: people who were out of the city, ill, or who did not appear to vote were all very obligingly "voted" by the machine. A woman who was visiting in Alabama registered a "machine" vote as did a veteran of World War I who had been confined for years to a Government hospital. There was also considerable violation of the secrecy of the ballot. The judges would open folded ballots and inspect them before putting them into the ballot boxes. Machine workers brooded over the voters' shoulders as they were marking their ballots. One precinct captain on the North Side who was actually a resident of the Country Club neighborhood registered for this primary from an address in the middle of a corn field in a praiseworthy attempt to identify his vote with the neighborhood in which he exercised authority.

The following statement obtained by the *Star* is typical of many. It is worth citing as an example of how the Pendergast machine "gets out the votes."

"On August 6, 1946, at about 6:45 p.m., I went to the polling place located in a radio shop in the 700 block on East Eighth Street. I went there to cast my vote at the primary election. I was met at the door by a man whom I would describe as about 5 feet 11 inches or 6 feet, having a large frame, and wearing glasses, white, about 180 pounds. I told him my name and that I wanted to vote. This man I judged to be a precinct worker. He was holding the poll book. He said, 'I voted you.' I said, 'How could you? Nobody could vote for me as no one knew how I wanted to vote.' I said, 'I haven't been here before today,' and he said, 'Nellie Rentie told me you weren't coming to vote.' Nellie Rentie is my apartment manager and she worked at the precinct on the primary election day. I told him I hadn't discussed this with Nellie. He said, 'Wait a minute,' and he went out and talked to some people in a car. Then he came back and asked me if I knew 'Lovey.' I told him I didn't. Later as we walked up the street this man pushed at me some folded bills. He handed these folded bills to me. I didn't take the money. As he handed me, or attempted to hand me, the money he said, 'Here take this and buy yourself some beer.' This all occurred as we were walking east on Eighth Street. This man then walked up the street and talked to Miss Rentie and told her I had been voted. I repeated to him and Miss Rentie that he had told me 'I voted you.' He said, 'Well we'll take care of you.' I told him I had missed my vote and expressed to him that I felt he had kept me from voting.

"As a consequence I was not allowed to cast my vote in the primary.

"These statements on this and the preceding page are true.

"SIGNED Estella R. Carter, 805 East Eighth Street,

fourth floor, front. Witnesses: John P. Swift, 909 East Forty-seventh Street; Dwight M. Smith, Jr., 916 Walnut."

In consequence of all that I have quoted and much more, the *Star* in its lead article for September 29, 1946, said among other things, "The bitter lesson learned by the 259 vote thieves who were prosecuted and punished as a result of their activities in 1936 apparently has been forgotten. The honest elections Kansas City has had in recent years are slipping back into the old patterns of poll booth chicanery." The *Star's* facts were gained from over 5,000 interviews. Fraud evidence was not collected from just one or two isolated cases. The *Star* pointed out that its purpose was to expose fraud, but that prosecution was the function of the Government. Therefore, when it turned over the evidence to the U. S. District Attorney it did so with the firm conviction that prompt and sweeping inquiry on the Government's part would be forthcoming.

The chairman of the Kansas City Board of Election Commissioners, Mr. Ludwick Graves, had called U. S. District Attorney Wear on the 16th of September, 1946, to arrange for a conference on the ground that there was some suspicion of fraud in the recent primary election. This conference took place the next day, and as a result District Attorney Wear telephoned the Department of Justice to inform that agency of a definite request by the Board of Election Commissioners for Government aid in investigating some rumored irregularity. In accordance with instructions received, District Attorney Wear wrote a letter to the Election Board assuring its members that on their provision of substantial evidence the Department of Justice would direct the FBI to make a complete and full investigation of the matter. So far so good. The City Council of Kansas City, Missouri, forwarded a resolution to Attorney-General Clark in Washington, to the U.S. District Attorney in Kansas City and to the Jackson County Prosecuting Attorney which requested immediate investigation of all violations of election laws at the primary, August 6, 1946, to the end that all persons guilty of violating Federal or State laws, or both, be prosecuted in the appropriate courts.

On top of all this, Mr. Jerome Walsh set up a cry to the special Committee on Campaign Expenditures of the House of Representatives, urging an investigation by their body. This investigation was made. The evidence obtained by it was turned over to the Attorney-General with a blunt statement that the facts in the report as submitted justified referral to the Department of Justice.

Meanwhile, it is fair to ask what was the position of the Federal Bureau of Investigation? Since 1941 by Department of Justice ruling the FBI was forbidden any longer to undertake investigations in cases involving denial of civil rights without the order of the Attorney-General. The FBI, therefore, was awaiting some sort of a directive. This came on October 11, 1946, in the form of a memorandum which in essence requested a "preliminary" investigation into the charges brought by the complainants. The joker in this lies in the word "preliminary," for it appeared on subsequent investigation that a "preliminary" report is little more than a check and appraisal of evidence already in hand from sources other than the well-known and efficient operations of the FBI. In his directive, the Attorney-General expressly limited the

FBI investigation to a questioning of persons designated by him, none of whom were persons suspected of crime, none of whom had first-hand knowledge of the alleged violations. In a word, the FBI was asked to check over the statements made by the Board of Election Commissioners and by the investigators employed by a private agency, the Kansas City *Star*. This once-over-lightly took a week.

On October 23rd, evidently suspecting that some wider extension was going to be given their work than its character would support, an agent of the FBI reminded his chief that U. S. District Attorney Wear was on notice that the report of the FBI investigation should not be cited to prove that further investigation was unnecessary.

The Attorney-General was requested by the FBI in a memorandum of October 25th to note that his precise orders had been followed and that further advice regarding full investigation was desired as soon as possible.

The U.S. District Attorney in Kansas City, Missouri, had not been idle. Shortly after he received his copy of the FBI's very limited findings (all of which he might have digested from the Kansas City *Star* some weeks before), he and his assistants prepared a twenty-three page review which purported to be a digest of the evidence brought to the attention of his office. The embarrassing incompleteness and inaccuracy of this review was not revealed until a later date, but it had served its purpose in the meanwhile. The U.S. District Attorney submitted a copy of this fallible document to each of the three Federal judges in Kansas City, Missouri, the Honorable A. L. Reeves, J. C. Collet and A. A. Ridge, and desired of them an opinion whether or no what they saw justified their calling into session a Federal Grand Jury. Since they accepted the review on its face value as a true synopsis of the available evidence, they were obliged to advise the U.S. District Attorney that they could find in it no evidence of a conspiracy.

Inasmuch as conspiracy is the basis for Federal prosecution of a vote fraud, it was then obvious that the U.S. Attorney was absolved from any obligation to proceed with the matter. At no time, however, did the judges absolve the State authorities or the County authorities from their duty to wade in and cast about them. Mr. Wear, armed with his impeccable opinion, given by men of appreciated probity, now wrote the Department of Justice that the district judges were unanimous in the opinion that there was not enough evidence to warrant a Grand Jury investigation of the alleged frauds. It would therefore follow that no further responsibility lay on the Department of Justice to follow through.

The Attorney-General, with what feelings I know not, ordered the files of the case closed on January 6, 1947, and somewhat gratuitously added that this was the result of a "thorough" investigation. I do not have to labor over exposing the thoroughness of the investigation insofar as the Federal authorities were concerned, nor do I have to point out to any of my readers the fact that the Kansas City *Star's* investigators, whose work lay at the base of this impressive pyramid, were untrained, were private persons, and were not engaged in searching for evidence of a conspiracy. Almost as an afterthought, may I remind you all that on November 5, 1946, the day of the general election, Mr. Axtell, President Truman's hand-picked candidate, was defeated at the polls by Albert L. Reeves, Jr., son of that veteran jurist whose courage and public spirit had availed so much in the investigation of the earlier frauds of 1936.

Almost at the very time that the Attorney-General was muzzling the bloodhounds, something very interesting was brewing in Jackson County. James J. Kimbrell, the newly elected Prosecuting Attorney of Jackson County, caused a County Grand Jury to be empanelled and began a vigorous investigation of alleged election irregularities and frauds committed in the 1946 primary.

Hundreds of witnesses were called before this body during the weeks that followed. The ballots and records of many precincts and wards were brought to the Grand Jury room, opened and carefully checked. Finally the ballots were recounted by the members of the jury. Judges and clerks of the election were subpoenaed and sworn to give evidence of what transpired in the polling places on election day. The registration books were examined for padding of ghost registrants and many persons listed as voters were called to give testimony. After weeks of gruelling work the County Grand Jury presented its final report to the Court, and with it returned indictments against seventy-one defendants.

In its final report the Grand Jury declared there was wholesale vote buying and bribery, that there was a miscount of votes in shocking proportions, that the evidence showed there "had been a deliberate and calculated plan to miscount votes and otherwise steal the election." The Jury, in its report, stated that the investigation convinced them that the candidate for Congress in the 5th Congressional District, Roger Slaughter, had been deprived of the nomination by a fraudulent miscount of votes and other types of fraud. The Jury concluded its report with the statement that the extent of fraud could be gauged only by scientific methods as employed by trained men. "There were definite indications of conspiracy and irregularities requiring such expert services bearing on the identity of handwriting, pencil marks, finger prints etc. It is general knowledge that the Federal Bureau of Investigation, United States Department of Justice has examiners and facilities to carry on such an investigation." The Jury strongly urged that the Department of Justice and the FBI enter the investigation.

The report of the Grand Jury was received on May 27, 1947, in the courtroom at Independence, Missouri. All ballots and records used by the jury in the investigation were returned to the vaults of the Kansas City Board of Election Commissioners for safekeeping.

By the time Slaughter himself had the benefit of the Grand Jury's evidence it was too late to contest the election. Slaughter told St. Louis *Star-Times* reporter Ralph O'Leary, on June 2, 1947, that the Kansas City Election Board in issuing credentials to official watchers and challengers in the 255 precincts of his district "gave practically all such posts to followers of the Pendergast machine, which was seeking my defeat at the order of President Truman . . . I sent an attorney, representing my campaign workers, to the election board to protest, but the board said the credentials had been distributed and it was too late to do anything about it. In each of the precincts where the grand jury has reported discovering vote frauds we had no representation."

When Slaughter made a statement to the effect that a political scandal of the first magnitude was brewing as a result of the Kansas City vote steal, President Truman was asked if he had any comment to make. The substance of his reply was that he had not seen the Slaughter statement, and that he attributed little significance to it considering the source. On July 11, 1947, the Washington *Evening Star* took this as a text for a stinging editorial entitled "Considering the Source." It said in part: "Now no one suggests that Mr. Truman, personally, had anything to do with the fraud, or that he personally approved of what was done. Still, the fact remains that the election was obviously stolen, and if it had been left to the Federal authorities nothing whatsoever would have been done about it. Furthermore, if Mr. Slaughter is right—and the President does not deny it—Mr. Truman continues to be a dues paying member of the Pendergast organization and permits that machine to list him on its letterhead as its vice-president. If the President is not going to let himself be worried by Mr. Slaughter as an individual, he nevertheless ought to be worried by the factual source from which Mr. Slaughter's criticism springs. The whole affair is a sordid business, the worst thing that can happen in a democracy, and the President, having enlisted the support of Pendergast in the first instance, cannot escape some measure of connection with it."

We must go back a little to pick up another thread. United States Senator James P. Kem of Missouri had been carrying on correspondence for some time with Attorney-

General Tom C. Clark, insisting that the Department of Justice investigate the election in Kansas City. In a letter dated January 14, 1947, Senator Kem reminded the Attorney-General that "Election irregularities by the Democratic political machine in Kansas City are an old story to Missouri voters who have a justifiable fear of the return of the dishonest election practices which were, for the time being, cleaned up by representatives of your Department several years ago. There has been no statement from your office since the report of the House committee was filed and since the FBI made its preliminary report."

In a speech in the Senate, May 20, 1947, Senator Kem said: "For years Kansas City has been disgraced by one of the most ruthless and corrupt political machines that ever besmeared American politics . . . Tom Pendergast, the leader of the machine, was sent to prison for income-tax evasion, and is now deceased, but the powerful machine he controlled and ruled, staggered and shaken by the imprisonment of so many of the henchmen, survived. Jim Pendergast, Tom's nephew and protege in machine politics, picked up the fallen reins of power and quietly bided his time to drive the machine back into full control of governmental affairs in Kansas City. Of course, the first and necessary step to control the community was to control the elections. By 1946, most of those who were convicted and imprisoned in the Federal penitentiary for vote frauds in the 1936 elections had served their terms or had been released by virtue of executive clemency, and were back in Kansas City."

The Attorney-General permitted the Senator to investigate the files of his Department, but in his answers to the Senator's letters he insisted that he could see no basis for Federal prosecution. The Senator rebutted this from the Attorney-General's own files with fifteen pieces of evidence of active fraud, and concluded his covering letter with a passionate reminder that the total and utter inaction of Federal officers in 1946 contrasted strangely with the attitude of Federal officers in similar circumstances ten years before. Nor was the Senator content with words. He submitted a resolution, Senate Resolution 116, which proposed an investigation by the Judiciary Committee of the Senate into the enforcement of Federal law with reference to the now notorious Missouri primary.

THE MILLS OF THE GODS

THE Senate inquiry requested by Senator Kem's Resolution did not propose to uncover new evidence of fraud. It was not intended to establish whether there had been violations of Federal law in the Kansas City, Missouri, primary election. The evidence collected by the Grand Jury of Jackson County and other agencies sufficed to establish the one, and as for the other, only thorough and scientific examination of the evidence could reveal conspiracy. It was hardly to be supposed that the poll watchers and election judges involved were going to make public announcement that they had conspired. Senator Kem's resolution proposed to examine the motives for apparent sloth and inactivity in the Department of Justice. In accordance with Senate procedure, the Judiciary Committee appointed a sub-committee to make a preliminary survey of the matter, with power to recommend a sweeping investigation should the findings warrant this. The first hearing was scheduled for the morning of May 28, 1947.

You will recall that on May 27, in the courthouse at Independence, Missouri, the sitting judge had received a full report from the Jackson County Grand Jury investigation into the vote frauds of August, 1946. The judge had thanked the members of the Grand Jury for their long, faithful service, and the jurors had gone away with the comfortable feeling that comes upon efficient discharge of civic duty. The evidence they had used to bring indictments against seventy-one persons was packed away in steel carrying cases and returned to the safe custody of the vault in the Kansas City courthouse, where two election commissioners, one Democrat and one Republican, sealed the cases.

In Washington, D. C., Senator Homer Ferguson, presiding as chairman of the sub-committee for preliminary scrutiny of the actions of the Department of Justice, began the hearings at a little before ten o'clock on Wednesday morning, May 28. After a few formal remarks in which he reminded the occupants of Room 424, Senate Office Building, why they were gathered together, he asked the Hon. Tom C. Clark, Attorney-General of the United States, to explain the inactivity of his Department. Attorney-General Clark was very much at his ease. He reminded the Sub-Committee (Senators Langer and McCarran were present, as was Senator Kem, who had come to see how his resolution would fare) that there was nothing easy about prosecuting a civil rights case, and cited numerous examples from his own experience and from the experience of the Department to prove it. Attorney-General Clark seemed sure of his ground that no conspiracy had been proved and that without proof of conspiracy no cases could be made out against defendants except under State law. What we may be permitted to call the hostile part of the Committee were quite prepared to admit this, but they reminded the Attorney-General that the provision of proof of conspiracy was as much his concern as anybody else's. In a word, that the Sub-Committee was interested in dereliction of duty and that he had been derelict. Attorney-General Clark then fell back on the contention that he "could only call them as he saw them" and that he was compelled to accept the findings of his subordinates in such matters. He desired to know if the members of the Sub-Committee imagined that he handled personally the hundreds of thousands of cases that were the work yearly of the Department of Justice.

To those who were following the hearing, it was apparent that Senator Kem was seething. He inquired of the Chairman whether he might ask the Attorney-General directly if he considered that specific testimony taken by the Senator from available Department of Justice files constituted proof of conspiracy on its face. Attorney-General Clark remarked that so far as he was concerned they could ask him anything. At this point the Chairman asked Senator Kem to reserve his question until all members of the Sub-Committee had been able to brief themselves on the point by reading the evidence in question. The Sub-Committee then went into executive session to review the evidence.

Upon resumption of open hearings, the Chairman announced that closing time was at hand and another hearing would be necessary. The Attorney-General hoped that the day be chosen so as not to interfere with his reception of an honorary degree in Texas on the second of June. No one appeared to have any objection to this. A genial mood settled down over the committee room, whether because the members felt magnanimous about making the Attorney-General's path easy, or because the mention of Commencement Day with its suggestions of bright juvenile hopes lifted the proceedings for a space above their somewhat questionable level. This happy mood lasted for about two minutes and a half.

While Senator Ferguson was requesting an aide to find some necessary papers, a telegram was delivered. Senator Kem ran his eye over it and handed it up to the chairman who scanned it and then hurriedly rapped for order.

"There has just been handed me a telegram dated May 28, ten A.M." he announced. "The telegram reads as follows: LAST NIGHT PRIMARY BALLOTS STOLEN FROM ELECTION COMMISSIONERS' VAULT."

It did not take very long for the implications of this piece of news to strike everyone in the room. The Attorney-General's mind was brought quickly back from academic honors to the hard and sordid present. After considerable milling about and random expression, Senator Kem was heard to say that he had verified the fact of the theft by telephoning Kansas City. The first meeting of the Sub-Committee ended then . . . sensationally, in a babble of outrage and good intentions.

Let us take a look at the circumstances in this latest of

Kansas City political crimes. The theft of the ballot boxes (and nothing else) was discovered at a little before eight o'clock on the morning of May 28. In no time at all, anxious Kansas City officials were staring at the battered steel doors of the forced vault and assuring one another that it was impossible.

But to the police it was plain that the doers of the deed had performed with great professional skill and had left nothing to chance. They had come fully prepared to blow the vault and they had done so. They had drilled the door to test its thickness; they had brought along a feather mattress to deaden sound. White cotton sacks had been hung over the lights within the vault, so that they would not shine in the darkness and give the alarm. No doors in the building had been forced except the vault door. There was no one to blame. The thieves seemed to have known the precise location of the impounded ballot boxes; a waste paper sack had been left conveniently in the vault so that it might serve to lug the loot away; the regular night watchman had gone on his vacation. Kansas City had been caught asleep at the switch.

The Chairman of the Election Board asked the FBI to take over the case immediately, but the Federal men replied, correctly, that they had no jurisdiction. It was reported unreliably around town that, on the night of the robbery, illegal Kansas City night clubs frequented by friends of the Pendergast machine had been the scene of many impromptu and inexplicable boozy celebrations. But despite prompt action by State and Kansas City police, no one was taken into custody.

Why were the ballots stolen? I don't have to answer

that question. Just remember that on their evidence, a Grand Jury had returned indictments against seventy-one persons. What a really scientific study of those ballots would have revealed can be now only the subject of conjecture.

How did the President of the United States react to this incident? "No comment" was his press secretary's answer to reporters. On the night of the ballot box theft the President was in a Kansas City hotel just a few blocks away. Whoever pulled the job showed little regard for the feelings of a man who had just made a trip to the bedside of his ailing mother.

The St. Louis *Post-Dispatch* of May 31, 1947, called the Clark-Truman inaction "A National Humiliation," in a stinging editorial.

Naturally enough the Sub-committee hearings subsequent to these larcenous goings-on in Kansas City were something of an anticlimax, but several interesting facts came out. At the second hearing, June 5, 1947, Mr. J. Edgar Hoover, Director of the Federal Bureau of Investigation, made it quite clear that his organization considered itself in no way bound to exceed directives from aloft. A detailed examination of the three Federal judges who had ruled unofficially that it was not necessary to impanel a Federal Grand Jury revealed what anyone might have guessed: that the judges regarded their opinions as friendly personal advice to the worried Mr. Wear rather than any exercise of their judicial function.

Mr. Wear himself appeared before the Sub-committee on June 6. It is fair to say that the attitude of the Committee Chairman towards Mr. Wear was somewhat hostile, and the exchanges between examiner and examinee had something of an Alice-in-Wonderland quality in their inconsequence and lack of point. Considerable time was taken up during Mr. Wear's examination in trying to find the originals of letters which Mr. Wear was presumed to have in a weird and wonderful file which accompanied him to the hearing room. Some of Mr. Wear's answers are interesting. Senator Kem at one point was disturbed over Mr. Wear's statement that suspicious circumstances did not necessarily justify an investigation. Senator Kem inquired whether Mr. Wear was still of that opinion. Mr. Wear replied that he had changed his mind since "these later developments."

Senator Kem: "What later development do you mean?"

Mr. Wear: "This burglary and larceny. That looks suspicious."

Senator Kem: "You mean after the ballots are stolen you think further investigation is justified?"

Mr. Wear then went on to say that he thought the loss of the ballots was not too important and that the members of the Jackson County Grand Jury, who had seen the ballots when they were still available, could give competent testimony in subsequent trials respecting the contents of the ballots. He did not appear worried over the loss of evidence that might be revealed under the microscope or by other scientific means. Mr. Wear reminded the Chairman that he was out of the city when the vault was broken open, adding, "I have an awfully good alibi."

He took strong issue with the testimony of the President of the Board of Election Commissioners that significant evidence had been supplied him by that body relative to its investigation of the vote frauds, and denied absolutely that his office could be held responsible for any investigations of crime until sufficient evidence was presented to it. There was some difference of opinion on this point. The examination of Mr. Wear wound up in a dispute over the commendation sent Mr. Wear by the Attorney-General's office for his "splendid co-operation" in the investigation of the disputed primary election. Senator Langer and Senator McCarran professing not to have any questions, the Chairman adjourned the hearing subject to call. There were no further meetings of the Sub-committee.

There were a few other interesting sidelights on the administration of the Department of Justice which developed in the course of the hearings. The Attorney-General had let it be inferred that instructions to the FBI in civil rights cases followed the pattern to be observed in the probe of the Slaughter-Axtell primary. Yet when instructions to the FBI in a similar case just across the river in Wyandotte County, Kansas, were examined by the Committee, it was found that no restrictions of any kind had been placed on the investigating agency. The Sub-committee was somewhat puzzled to know which was the rule and which was the exception.

By the first of June the Attorney-General, upon whose nervous system the ballot theft seemed to have exercised considerable effect, had set in motion two FBI investigations; one into the theft of the ballots, the other a "full" investigation of election frauds in the Slaughter-Axtell primary. The newspapers, in commenting on the Attorney-General's zeal, seemed to agree with FBI Director Hoover's remark before the Sub-committee that the loss of the ballots must seriously handicap the efforts of FBI agents. President Truman issued a statement to the effect that the vote fraud cases should be carried to their logical conclusion. With the vital evidence gone, there was not much doubt what the logical conclusion would be.

Senator Kem, whose function as the plumed knight of good government had become established by now, engaged in a long and bitter contest within the Senate to force resumption of committee hearings on his resolution. In radio addresses, speeches in the Senate, and releases to the press, he endeavored to force action before the closing of the session. He had had enough experience with the public memory to know that the task would be doubly difficult in a new session. On July 25 it was apparent that the Senate was deadlocked on the matter. The Republican majority carried a first vote which tabled a motion to delay the investigation until the next year. Senator Taft announced to the embattled Senators that he was prepared to stay all night until the Kem resolution was disposed of. Senator Ferguson, speaking from the floor, claimed that his inquiry had established a *prima facie* case against the Attorney-General, and somewhat sarcastically observed that it would hardly be fair to the Administration not to clear the good name of its Attorney-General before other business was taken up.

A good deal of the difficulty which the Kem resolution encountered in the Senate arose out of the Sub-committee's refusal to report the resolution out to the full Committee. Senator Langer of North Dakota was responsible for this. He gave as his reason for refusing to report the resolution that the Attorney-General, so far as he could see, was damned if he did and damned if he didn't. Supposing that the Attorney-General had taken immediate and positive action in the first stages of the vote fraud case, would not those who were anxious to make him look bad be able to claim that he had stepped into the case and taken over the evidence for sinister purposes? This was Senator Langer's reason for refusing to report. The Democratic high command, however, used the Senator's scruples to good advantage, and proposed for discussion in the Senate a pending veterans' bill as being of more immediate consequence than a vote scandal in a single county or a single city.

Not to waste too much time with the details of Senatorial maneuver, the Kem resolution found itself lost in a woods of words. A polite filibuster began. Not one of the old swashbuckling, Bible-reading type, but a gentle refusal on the part of Democratic speakers to discuss the matter. They were perfectly willing to talk on anything else and did. Senator Hatch held forth eloquently on the rehabilitation of Europe, on British military policy in Palestine, on salmon fishing, and various other subjects. During all this, there was continual needling from Senator Kem and Senators Wherry and Ferguson. As the wilting evening drew to a close, Senator Kem asked Senator Barkley directly whether he proposed to continue the same tactics on the following day. Mr. Barkley replied that he could not say, but that he found the topics treated very interesting and proposed to have something to say himself.

Faced with the prospect of a real filibuster on the pending motion, and considering the tall pile of bills which awaited action before adjournment, Senator Robert A. Taft rose up in the angry confusion of the Senate chamber and very reluctantly delivered the *coup de grace* to the proposed inquiry. The Senate glumly tackled a great mass of routine, and Senator Kem proclaimed over the radio that a small clique of Democrats was thwarting the public's will by imposing an iron curtain between the eyes of justice and the facts. So on June 26, 1947, ended the first phase of the great inquiry. May I insist that the problem involved in Senator Kem's resolution was not the direct point at issue. The defeat of the resolution, therefore, does not affect the issue of honest elections one way or another. It merely proves that disciplined party action in a legislative body can block an inquiry into dishonest elections and can protect a public official against the effects of his own negligence.

EPILOGUE

Epilogue

AS I write these words, Congress is sitting. Whether the 1946 primary fraud in Kansas City, Missouri, is to be the subject of new inquiry and debate I do not know. I am prepared to admit that of itself it is a matter much less important than foreign policy and domestic economy, but if it is viewed not of itself but as a symptom of civic disease, then I must say that it is of the utmost importance that we examine it.

How shall we stand before the world and preach the good and the truth in Democracy if such perversions of the Democratic process are regarded by us as trivial or the subject for the loud laugh that speaks the vacant mind? I should like to sound a hopeful note at the end of this book, but unless we can count on a government which will devote itself to the extermination of minor bossism, we shall go on having Pendergast machines and vote frauds until some machine bigger, more intelligent, and more corrupt than all the others will win control of this country and topple us in our pride. All such a machine will need will be another Huey Long. In almost every community in America there is at least one man ready to corrupt the machinery of elections if he knows that he will be protected higher up. The smallness of a boss or of a machine is no reason for us to minimize his or its potentialities. A corrupt village election is as much a threat to our Democracy as was the arrogant grip of Huey Long on an entire State.

Tom Pendergast started in the West Bottoms of Kansas City, but before he went to prison his hand pulled almost every string in the State of Missouri. A civic disease of this kind cannot be contained or cured by the kind of local quarantine and method of treatment prescribed by Attorney-General Clark. The inherent moral worth of the human personality is expressed in our government, and those conditions essential to the proper expression of the moral worth of the community are the things we call our civil rights. The ballot, the honest ballot, is the one weapon with which the average citizen is provided to defend his liberty. Corrupt it and you leave him defenseless.

The earlier chapters of this book have shown bossism in its true colors, a complex of greed, crime and ignorance. No apologist can refute the facts. I am not interested, and you should not be, in the hypocrisy which proclaims that the corruptions of the machine in politics may be excused because slickness of administration is to be preferred to honest fumbling. Nor am I interested in the equally specious claim that under the rule of a machine the poor are fed out of the spoils of the rich. In Tom Pendergast's case, the relative poverty of race track touts and bookmakers may have been assuaged, but the slums showed no sign of amelioration.

The right to vote in an honest election, the struggle for the secrecy of the ballot, these are our heritage. They are the result of a long, uphill battle. They must not be carelessly lost, for, aside from the immediate ill effects of dishonest elections, in the long-range view the faith of the electorate in Democratic processes is undermined by such crimes against the ballot. That is the real tragedy. In the Democratic form of government the individual is paramount. The vote that he casts has about it something sacred, and I use this word with due deliberation.

If you want to see the true apotheosis of machine government, easy government, "efficient" government in the sense that machine politicians use these words, look to Soviet Russia and to the Fascist systems of Germany and Italy. In them the individual was and is nothing. He is a serf to the all-powerful State. His life is its pawn. And I need not remind you that the first step in the building of these slave states was the prostitution of the democratic election. That is why it is so important for us to purify our elections. We cannot do this by making speeches. We cannot do it even by resolutions in the Senate and inquiries into negligence. We cannot do it by sitting on our own front porches and shouting, "Kick the rascals out!" We can do it only by ourselves entering the fight, sharing in our own politics, guaranteeing by our presence and action that we have honest and intelligent men in office, elected properly and honestly. Eternal vigilance is the price of liberty—your vigilance, my vigilance. The picnics and the hand-outs, the brass bands and the charities of ward bosses and political clubs are not acceptable unless you are aware who is footing the bill. Let us have no more statues or public eulogies on the "Blubberlip Bills" or "Gas-House Charlies" or other paunchy gluttons at the public trough. Audit the books, ask for an accounting, keep eternal watch.

We stand now in a time when we must revise much of our traditional thinking. Especially is this true in the realm of economics. Some of our largest cities are today bankrupt. Many more are on the verge of bankruptcy. A contributing cause, if not the main cause, is political graft. It was not for nothing that Viscount Bryce called attention to the evils of municipal politics, or that Lincoln Steffens titled his exposé, "The Shame of The Cities." Over too many years, too many political pirates have raided municipal treasuries or have debauched honest city finances by their easy-going methods of bookkeeping. In the loose frontier days there was enough boodle to go around, and our cities flourished despite the thieves. But the honeymoon is over now. Public indifference to the highhanded practices of predatory political gangs brought this about. The average voter in a large city feels that he is helpless to do anything about situations like this. Ignorance and apathy play into the hands of the boss. The citizen forgets that HE is the Government. This elementary concept escapes too many of us.

Boss rule has come to be looked upon as an American tradition. Edward J. Flynn, Democratic boss of the Bronx in New York City, a man high in the councils of his party, recently wrote a book designed to prove that bosses are a product of our political philosophy; he makes a great point of showing that there are good bosses as well as bad ones. He tries to show that bosses have the political experience and grasp of community affairs necessary to real leadership. These benevolent despots are really concerned with the welfare of the people. They know better than the people themselves what is good for them. Up to a certain point Boss Flynn is right. Most political bosses have undoubted leadership, they almost invariably have great knowledge of human nature, most of them have worked their way up from humble beginnings. Tom Pendergast fits this description. When the going was tough it was comforting to know that you had Tom Pendergast on your side. It was almost as good as an insurance policy. It was protection. The fallacy in this type of thinking is in assuming that the boss does good *per se*. The goodness of the boss is always discriminatory. He does good when and where it is most expedient. His benefactions are coldly calculated. If his motives were unselfish and humanitarian he could do an equal amount of good without being a boss, and could accumulate wealth and prestige by honest means. Clean government is so simple most people miss it. All we need, to have it in any community, is honestly elected officials who have the moral courage to abide by their oaths of office when tempted to violate them. When that happens bossism comes to an end. Strictly speaking bossism is not within the law. When a Hague says "I am the law" he is really saying "I am above the law."

The ballot—in the party caucus, in the primary, and in the elections—is the weapon. It can be used in many ways. One can vote right and one can vote wrong. It is possible for whole sections of the country to vote inexpediently on some issues. Just having a certain number of people called Republicans and a certain number of people called Democrats is not the object of suffrage. Suffrage is the badge of freedom. The thing that is important is the right to vote, the privilege of exercising our free choice. When that right is denied us, corrupted or tampered with, honor and decency pass from our public life. Those who associate with vote-stealers betray the confidence of the people.

I have faith in democracy. I have faith in the American people. We put up with a lot of political graft, inefficiency and skulduggery, and then we get good and mad and clean house. We amuse ourselves with political conventions, parades, and all the circus trappings of political high-jinks. They have entertainment value, like the World Series. The politicians do not take these things too seriously. Neither do the voters. In our politics we dispense with revolutions, the coup-d'etat, duels and the student riots of more volatile peoples, contenting ourselves with orderly processes. We smile at stories of "nominations in smoke-filled rooms." We are amused when we hear that some ward boss has "traded off" his votes in return for three good jobs in the Department of Street Cleaning. Boys will be boys. When we find out that a paving contract has brought double what it should because of certain "arrangements" of a political nature, we shrug it off. We're rich; we can afford it. A more volatile people might rise in anger, form a mob and burn the City Hall. We're Americans; we don't do such things.

Then one fine day we wake up to discover that hired thugs have walked off with our ballot boxes. Suddenly the truth hits us. This isn't funny. "Stop, thief! That's my vote you're stealing." And now is the time, if ever, for action. For otherwise, arrogance breeds arrogance, success breeds success, and it will not be too long before a fellow you've never seen will walk up to you on election day, thrust a gun in your face and tell you how to vote. "Just say 'yes,' bud." Being an American, you're not going to like it.

I end my book with a quotation from highest authority. William Marcy Tweed in 1871, the great Boss Tweed, an earlier "friend of the poor," remarked: "As long as **I** count the votes, what are you going to do about it?"

What are *you* going to do about it?